What Others Are Sa

MW00655599

"The oil of laughter cools the engine of our overheated lives and keeps us from burning up in an anxious heap of unhappiness. Can you imagine how dismal it would be to live in a world without laughter? Jim Harvey can't and he doesn't want you to either! He thinks laughter is God's gift to us, and so do I! Read this lovely little book in honor of laughter and you will laugh more and live better!"

Dr. Timothy Brown
President, Western Theological Seminary
Reformed Church in America, Holland, Michigan

"Does God Laugh? will give you something to think about and something to smile about. It creatively explores a quality of God's personality that is often overlooked. It calls us to enjoy humor at its best."

Dr. Wayne Schmidt
Senior Pastor, Kentwood Community Church
Grand Rapids, Michigan

"Wit and wisdom are twin tools that God uses to tickle and teach us. Dr. Harvey shows how He does that in this new volume that will both entertain and enlighten. Be prepared to laugh and learn."

Dr. Douglas Norwood
Executive Director, Broken Jars Ministry,
Allentown, Pennsylvania

"We all enjoy laughing. It's good for you. Dr. Harvey's book will encourage you. May the joy of the Lord fill you. 'The joy of the Lord is your strength (Nehemiah 8:10).' "

The Right Reverend Robert Allen Iobst
Bishop of the Moravian Church in America
Winston-Salem, North Carolina

"A man was supposed to pick up a minister at the airport, but he had no idea of what he looked like. When he saw a rather somber looking fellow in a dark suit, he figured he had found his man. He asked, 'Are you Rev. Jones?' 'No', the man replied, 'I'm not a minister. My arthritis just makes me look like this way.' This book dispels the notion that Christians must be somber people, and encourages us to treasure laughter as one of God's gifts."

Pastor George Vander Weit
Senior Pastor, Fuller Avenue Christian Reformed Church
Grand Rapids, Michigan

Does God Laugh?

*Can a Serious God
Have a Sense of Humor?*

L. James Harvey, Ph.D.

Does God Laugh?
Can a Serious God Have a Sense of Humor?
Copyright ©2008 L. James Harvey, PhD

Published by Harvest Day Books, an imprint of Book Marketing Solutions, LLC.

Unless otherwise indicated, scripture quotations are from the Holy Bible, New International Version (NIV).

The animal pictures in Chapter 4 have come from the following sources:
Personal photos of the author L. James Harvey.
The internet web site of the U.S. Government Fisheries and Wildlife Service (www.fws.gov) These pictures are in the Public Domain.
The following organizations/photographers and are used with their permission as noted.
San Diego Zoo
Brent Huffman, Ultimate Images Ungulate
Michael Turco
The cartoons in Chapter 6 are used with the permission of the following:
Peanuts – United Media Reprint Rights
BC – John L. Hart FLP and Creators Syndicate Inc.
Glasbergen Cartoons – Randy Glasbergen, Cartoonist

Harvey, L. James.
    Does God laugh? : Can a serious God have a sense of humor / L. James Harvey, PhD. -- Traverse City, Mich. : Harvest Day Books, 2008.
        v. ; cm.
        ISBN: 978-1-934792-03-2
        1. God (Christianity)--Attributes. 2. Philosophical theology.
        I. Title.
BT130 .H37 2008
231.4--dc22   0807

This book is available at ReadingUp.com

Dedication

This book is dedicated to the LIGHThouse Adult Bible Class of the Kentwood Community Church in Grand Rapids, Michigan. Under the able leadership of Bill and Virginia Campbell, each Sunday this class is filled with important Bible study, challenges to serve and support Christian missions, and laughter. The LIGHThouse ABC has been a joyous place to learn, serve, and laugh, and that's a great combination.

The book is also dedicated to all those wonderful Christian friends I've been blessed with down through the years with whom I have swapped some wonderful stories and hardy laughs. You have enriched and extended my life, and have inspired this book. I thank you.

Contents

Acknowledgements

A number of people have been helpful in shaping this book. The following people read early manuscripts and offered their advice and encouragement.

Rev. Chester Droog

Mr. Kurt Gearhart

Rev. Don Hoffman

Rev. Vern Hoffman

The Rt. Rev. Robert Iobst

Mr. Mike Miller

Dr. Doug Norwood

Mr. Fred and Charlcie Olivier

Dr. Wayne Schmidt

Rev. Daniel Smith

Pastor George Vander Weit

As with all my writing, a special thanks goes to my exceptional editor of first resorts, Jackie, my wife of 56 years and my best friend.

Preface

Does God have a sense of humor? Does he ever laugh? Does he have a lighter side? Can we really know in this life what God is like? Does he ever give us clues regarding what he's like? I believe the answers are yes, yes, yes, yes, and yes.

We all have some concept which comes to mind when the name God is mentioned. The concept may be wrong or incomplete, yet it is nevertheless in our minds and it affects the way we react to God and issues relating to life, faith, and the life beyond. But where did that concept come from? Is it anywhere near correct?

From birth we begin to pick up ideas about all kinds of things, and as we mature we pick up thoughts and ideas relating to what God is like. These ideas come from our parents, teachers, significant others, pastors, etc. As we grow older, the concept of God is further shaped by our education, experiences, and the world around us.

If we are members of a religion, that faith will help us shape our concept of God. Christians believe God reveals himself to us through the Bible, through the life of Jesus, through others, and through the Holy Spirit. But is our concept of God, whatever it is, complete? Possibly not! Come with me on a brief journey, where we will explore just one small aspect of God's character. The journey, I hope, will be interesting, meaningful, and fun. I ask you to go on this trip because it has been my experience that the part of God's nature we will examine here has been overlooked, or at best downplayed by most faith traditions.

Does God have a sense of humor? Let's take a look and see if we can determine whether he does. My fondest wish is that the reader of this book will conclude God indeed has a sense of humor and certainly laughs. My hope also is that the reader, coming to this conclusion, will find they are drawn into an even closer relationship with this most complex and wonderful God. Eternity will certainly be a joyous and fun place to be if the thesis of this book holds true.

The Reason for the Question

Is there something missing in the average person's perception of God? I believe there may be. That's why this book was written. It is critical for people to have a proper understanding of God's nature — at least as close to the truth as we humans can get. That perspective will form the foundation of our relationship with God, or determine whether, in fact, we have an association with God at all. It is clear that people's views of God cover a wide range of possibilities. Is God a fearsome judge? Is he a loving Santa Claus? Is he approachable? Is he somber and strict or kind and loving? This book was written to hopefully bring a special focus on one aspect of God's character — his sense of humor.

It would be presumptuous of me, or of any mortal, to believe we could comprehend and define the full character of God. Even learned theologians can't do this (it doesn't keep them from trying, however) because we are all limited in our mental and experiential capabilities.

Let us begin by acknowledging that God is far beyond our power to fully comprehend. He is eternal, we are mortal. He is the Creator, we are the created. He is omniscient, we are mentally restricted. He is perfect, we are sinful. He is omnipotent, we are weak and limited. Once we make these statements, however, we can also say God has chosen to reveal aspects of his character to us so we can have some understanding of him.

We need to understand from the beginning that our comprehension of God and his revelation of himself to us are limited by our ability to comprehend the messages he sends our way. For example, God has chosen to reveal himself to us as our heavenly Father. The concept of "father" has meaning to us because we have earthly fathers, and we know what characteristics a perfect father should have. At the same time, we know that God is not our father in the same sense as are our earthly fathers. God's relationship to us is much different. In addition, the term father connotes to us a male sexual identity, yet we may readily speculate, based on other information about heaven (i.e., in Luke 20:35, Jesus says in heaven, there is no marriage), that God may well be sexless, or a complete entity who is fully male and female. God clearly seems to be far beyond our human understanding.

In discussions about Jesus with some Moslem friends, they say Jesus, while one of the greatest prophets and teachers, cannot be the Son of God because God is far above human beings (and our sexual natures) and therefore cannot and did not have a son. In that they are partially correct. God did not conceive Jesus with Mary, in the way we understand human reproduction. God in his majesty and omnipotence, however, had the power to come to earth in human form through an immaculate conception. God, in communicating his love for us, set an example that we can all understand because we can know what a sacrifice it would be for any father to watch his only son, who was blameless, suffer and die for someone else. In short, God in his wisdom and omnipotence chose the father-son relationship and Jesus' sacrifice to communicate his love to us through a medium we could understand. Therefore I would say to my Moslem friends, if God is as great and all-powerful as they believe he is, then he certainly has the power to do what Christians believe he did in Jesus Christ.

This Moslem/Christian debate about Jesus simply leads to the argument I posit above, namely, God can only communicate to us in a framework we can understand, meaning those things in our world with which we are familiar and of which we have some knowledge. God does communicate to us about himself, and we all, in our own way, do have a concept of God in our mind. The concepts are formed through a number of sources and with whatever information comes to us from our personal, educational, and religious experiences.

One of the reasons I wrote this book is I come out of a Calvinistic heritage, which I believe, in hindsight, painted an incomplete picture of the character of God or at least tended to overemphasize the harsher characteristics of God's nature and downplay the more likeable aspects. God was presented to me from childhood as a somber God of power, wisdom, and judgment. He was a God who could and did get angry, and who was ready to sentence people to an everlasting hell if they failed to love and serve him. He was also put forth as a God of love and forgiveness, but the judgment, wrath, joyless legalism, and hellfire seemed to edge out the more positive characteristics. Yet I never remember God being presented as one who had a sense of humor, or who laughed. It is clear many theologians consider presenting God as one who laughs or has a sense of humor, would tend to diminish the seriousness of faith, and the life and death struggle between good and evil we are in here on earth. They may be right, but they can also easily offer a harsh and bland view of God that can hide the joy and pleasure of a true, comprehensive faith.

I believe the Quakers, Calvinists, and other conservative Protestant groups who came to settle America tended to believe humor was too close to wickedness, and that laughing and merriment tended to detract from the seriousness of life. Robert Barclay, a Quaker, wrote in a 1676 document entitled *Apology for the True Divinity*, that Christians "should shun everything not most serious and grave, including laughing, sporting, gaming, mockery, and jesting." He further indicated that these things are "not harmless."

The Puritans and their piety, and John Calvin and his weighty doctrine all seemed to play into the picture I painted for me as I was growing up, namely, that faith was a kind of legalistic system full of fear, and that life was a continual battle to avoid God's judgment and hell. It's almost as if, without intentionally doing so, pastors and theologians presented Christianity as a joyless, pleasureless journey through life with a harsh judgmental God waiting for us when we died. The positive, loving side of God was presented, too, but seemed to be minimized for fear that if it predominated, Christians would be inordinately tempted to sin, knowing God's love and grace would allow earthly pleasures at little or no risk.

There seems to be a strain of Christianity which has purposely avoided laughter and pleasure because it is, as Barclay concluded above, "not harmless." Saint John Chrysostum, a first century Christian leader, is reported to have preached a sermon against laughter and playfulness in 390 AD because he said, "They were too close to paganism and this world." Erma Bombeck, the now deceased comedienne extraordinaire, said at one time, "There is a tradition of solemnity in Christianity." She was right, and maybe that is good and necessary, but maybe the pendulum has swung too far in one direction and needs to come back a bit to the center.

Dr. Robert Schuller, the popular TV preacher and founder of the *Hour of Power* and Crystal Cathedral, comes from the same Calvinistic background as I do — the Reformed Church in America (RCA). In his autobiography (*My Journey*. HarperCollins, 2002), Schuller indicates that his whole ministry, which focuses heavily on "possibility thinking," has been in large part an attempt to overcome the negative impact Calvinism and a misunderstood concept of "total depravity" has had on people. Parenthetically, I should add that Schuller, who has studied Calvin in-depth, feels John Calvin's beliefs were not fully understood, and were miscommunicated down through the years by his followers. In short, Schuller blames Calvin's followers for the joyless, somber, shaming, blaming form of Christianity that has too often characterized those who follow his teachings (Schuller 2002, 99).

It might be further added that I have often wondered whether this "drab Calvinism" wasn't one reason the RCA has produced two of the country's greatest positive thinkers of the 20th century. Dr. Norman Vincent Peale, who wrote the classic *The Power of Positive Thinking*, and was pastor of the Marble Collegiate Church in New York City, which is affiliated with the RCA, was and is internationally associated with "positive thinking." Peale was a role model and supporter of Dr. Schuller's ministry. In some ways, Schuller took Peale's "positive thinking," turned it into "possibility thinking," and planted it on the West Coast in the 1950s in a rapidly growing Orange County, California. Peale and Schuller became what one RCA member called "RCA's positive bookends," one on each coast of the U.S., trying to undue some of the negative aspects of Calvinism by preaching a positive psychology, inspiring people to develop a healthy self-esteem, and introducing a new upbeat version of God and Christianity.

All Christians have at one time or another heard people refer to "the God of the Old Testament" and "the God of the New Testament" as if there were two different Gods. Usually, these references portray the God of the Old Testament as a harsh, rigid, somber, judgmental God who majored in punishing people when they made mistakes, while the God of the New Testament was a God of love and forgiveness. Our minister gave a persuasive sermon some time ago on this very subject, where he carefully documented from both New and Old Testaments that God hasn't changed at all. The character traits revealed in the Old Testament are all there in the New Testament as well. In fact, if we believe the Bible, then God and Jesus are "the same yesterday, today, and forever (Hebrews 13:8)." It is clear that Jesus provides a more detailed look at God incarnate, and from him we can get a clearer picture of some of God's characteristics, but even so, those characteristics of God haven't changed at all.

This book is not an attempt to dissect the doctrines of Calvin or the Christian church. Nor is it an attempt to construct a theological treatise on the character of God. It is an attempt to seek out one element of God's character, which I believe has been overlooked and underestimated. It seems clear after some study of the subject that God does have a sense of humor and he does indeed laugh, if we just look at the evidence. It's also evident that when we see the facts, we do get a more balanced and favorable picture of our Heavenly Father. We also get a somewhat different view of heaven: streets of gold, yes; singing, yes; joy, yes; but laughter, too!

This book, by the way, is not the first to approach this subject. Others, perhaps burdened as I have been with the absence of the humorous side of God, have written books such as *The Humor of Christ* (Elton Trueblood. Harper & Row, 1964), *Humor: God's Gift* (Tal D. Bonham. Broadman Press, 1987), *The Joyful Christ* (Cal Samara. Harper & Row, 1985), and *God Created Laughter* (Conrad Hyers. John Knox Press, 1987). This list is not exhaustive, and the treatment of God and humor has been addressed by many others in articles and chapters of books. It simply reinforces the fact that it is a topic of interest and one I felt needed to be revisited on my faith journey at this time in history, with the thought it might be of help to others as well.

In approaching this subject, a number of topics will be covered, including:

- What do we find on the subject in the Bible?
- What can we learn from Jesus?
- What do we learn from observing Christian leaders?
- What does recent research teach us about the characteristics and impact of laughter?
- What humor do we find in God's creation?
- And is there humor in the church?

In addition, this book will conclude with a brief overview of American humor, which I believe is unique. In Appendix A, the reader will be treated to some laughs from material I have collected over a lifetime. Hopefully, this material will provide evidence of the kind of laughter God intends for our benefit and good health. Lastly, in Appendix B, I will deal with a controversial topic in Christian circles namely, is the popular phenomenon of "holy laughter," considered by some to be a manifestation of the Holy Spirit, really holy?

What Does the Bible Say?

If we believe the Bible is the inspired and revealed word of God, then it is natural for us to look there for any indications that God has a sense of humor. Does the Bible say God has a sense of humor, and that he laughs? Yes, it does.

The most direct passage is in Psalms 2:4 (all scriptural references are from the NIV), where we read, "The one enthroned in heaven laughs; the Lord scoffs at them." Here the psalmist, David, the son of Jesse and King of Israel, prophesies regarding Jesus' coming and the forces of evil that will come against him and his kingdom. The evil forces will be defeated and the psalmist says that God (the one enthroned in heaven) laughs at them. God, in essence, laughs at their defeat and foolishness. The psalmist says directly here that God laughs.

In Psalm 59:8, we find something quite similar. In this passage, psalmist David is ruminating about his enemies and their eventual defeat, and in verse 8 he says, "But you, O Lord, laugh at them; you scoff at all the nations." Again in Psalm 37:13 we read, "But the Lord laughs at the wicked, for he knows their day is coming."

So in three cases David not only indicates God laughs, but in each case he indicates God will laugh at the defeat of evil forces.

There is one other passage in the Bible that shows God laughs. In Job 41:29 we read, "A club seems to him but a piece of straw, he laughs at the rattling of the lance." In this verse, God is laughing at those who would threaten him.

These are the only four biblical passages I know of where we read directly that God laughs. If they were the only evidence of God's sense of humor, given the many pages in the Bible, I would find it quite unsatisfactory. Besides, in all four cases God is laughing at the demise of the forces of evil— hardly a strong indication of a sense of humor, as we think of it. Fortunately, there is a wealth of evidence in addition to these four direct references to support the concept of God having a sense of humor.

For instance, in the book of Genesis, we get a glimpse of God's sense of humor. It relates to God promising Abraham that he will bless him with a son, though Abraham was 100 and Sarah, his wife, was 90. When God promised Abraham a son, we read in Genesis 17:17 that "Abraham laughed." Later, when Sarah overheard God again promising to give Abraham a son, she too laughed (Genesis 18:12). It is obvious God knew they both were amused by the idea that they could have a son at their advanced age. We also get a glimpse of God's sense of humor in the naming of the new son. God says to Abraham in Genesis 17:19 that he should name his son Isaac. The name Isaac literally means, "he laughs." In effect, I believe God said, "Okay, Abraham and Sarah, if you're going to laugh at my promise of a son at your advanced age, you'll name your son Isaac so that every time you call his name you'll be reminded that you laughed and doubted me when I made you this promise." Is this proof of God's sense of humor? Maybe yes, maybe no, but I believe it is.

In Luke 6:21, we read the words of Jesus as he states in the Beatitudes,

"Blessed are you who weep now, for you will laugh." Jesus says we will laugh — when? — in heaven. If there's laughter in heaven, can we imagine that God or Jesus will not be involved? I can't.

I believe there's another instance of God's humor in the Bible, in I Kings 18. Here we have Elijah challenging 450 prophets of the pagan god Baal to a contest on Mt. Carmel to prove who the true god was, Baal or the God of Israel. Elijah proposed that they build altars and call upon their respective gods to send fire to burn up the sacrifice. The prophets of Baal agreed and Elijah offered to let them go first. After they built their altar, the prophets called upon Baal to send fire. No fire came, and after several hours Elijah showed some humor by saying to the prophets, "Shout louder, . . . surely he is a god! Perhaps he is deep in thought or busy, or traveling. Maybe he is sleeping and must be awakened (I Kings 18:27)." Elijah poked fun at the prophets of Baal before he set up his altar and God sent down fire to prove he was the true God. Did Elijah, one of the greatest prophets in the Bible, have a sense of humor? I think so, but there's much more.

One word that is used throughout the Bible in conjunction with God, heaven, and the spirit-filled Christian life is the word *joy*. The word joy is used some 800 times in the Bible. Now joy is defined in *Webster's New World Dictionary* in the following ways: 1. a very glad feeling; happiness; great pleasure; delight 2. anything causing such a feeling 3. the expression or sharing of such a feeling. Joy is not the same thing as humor or laughter, but they are closely related. Healthy humor and laughter produce joy and many other positive outcomes, as we shall see later. It is fair to assume that one who is full of joy will often smile or laugh. It is also fair to assume that if those in heaven rejoice and are full of joy, as stated in the Bible (Romans 14:17, I Peter 4:13, Luke 15:7 and 10), then joy and laughter are a part of the character of God. Can anyone with any concept of heaven at all imagine a place where happiness, joy, and laughter are not an important part of the landscape? Frankly, I cannot.

The prophet Isaiah, in Isaiah 12:3, in effect says that joy is a characteristic of God, and reinforces the idea that heaven is full of joy (Isaiah 44:23). Therefore, it's fair to assume heaven is full of joy too, that joy is part of the character of God, and that humor and laughter can and often cause joy and flow from it.

No one has written more about heaven lately than Randy Alcorn. His book entitled *Heaven* (Tyndale Publishers, Inc., 2004) is a classic in the field. Alcorn indicates he has read about 150 books on heaven before writing his, so he knows what other religious authors think about God and the hereafter. Alcorn says, "God won't only wipe away all tears, he'll fill our hearts with joy and our mouths with laughter (Alcorn 2004, 409)." Alcorn further states one of Satan's greatest lies is that while God and Christianity are joyless and humorless, he and evil are the only forces conveying real pleasure and happiness. Alcorn's right! He summarizes his position by saying, "We need a biblical theology of humor that prepares us for an eternity of celebration and spontaneous laughter (Alcorn, 409)." Amen to that!

I suppose there are some who might say in heaven the peace and joy we will experience will be so deep, prevalent, and conditioned by the presence of God that laughter and humor will not be needed to help produce or enhance our basic joy. I can't really argue with that point, and can only say time will tell. I can say, however, if we look at some other evidence, it becomes crystal clear God has a sense of humor.

Human Nature

In Genesis 1:27 we read "God created man in his own image." If this is true, we humans can perform a simple task of reverse engineering and come to a clear conclusion: If we can laugh and have a sense of humor, then by deduction, so can God, since we are created in his image. But we don't have to stop there because God came to earth in Jesus Christ. By taking a close look at Jesus, we can get additional proof regarding this aspect of God's character. So let's take a better look at Jesus.

Humor in Jesus

If we believe Jesus was the Son of God and was God incarnate, as I do, then in looking at Jesus we get a direct reflection of some of the characteristics of God the father. Did Jesus laugh? Did he have a sense of humor? Obviously, he did!

First of all, Jesus was human as well as divine. As a human, he had the same emotions we have. Jesus wept over Lazarus (John 11:35), showing sorrow. He demonstrated anger when he threw the money-changers out of the Temple (John 2:14 and Matthew 21:12-13). If Jesus had the full range of emotions, as I believe he did, then he experienced joy and laughter along with other emotions. But can we find evidence of his laughter and humor specifically in the Bible? Yes, we can!

What we do not find in the Bible is a list of jokes told by Jesus. His humor was much more subtle and complex. Does this mean Jesus never told a joke? I doubt it. I'm sure he did, but the Bible does not cover very much of what Jesus said and did over the course of his life. We know about his birth, about an incident when he was 12 years old, and very little else until his three-year public ministry commenced when he was about 30 years old. Even during his public ministry, most of what he said and did is not recorded. Only critical events and conversations are recorded as the thread of God's redemptive work unfolded through the life, ministry, crucifixion, and resurrection of Jesus.

We do, however, learn some things about Jesus. For example, we learn that the first miracle he performed was at a wedding feast in Cana. Here, Jesus turned the water into wine (John 2:1-11). Now, at the risk of making some of my good Baptist friends angry, let's take a look at what happened. Wedding feasts in those times were really good parties. They went on for several days. A lot of wine was consumed at these marriage feasts, and the practice was to serve the best wine at the beginning. By the second or third day, attendees had typically lost the ability to distinguish the good wine from the poor wine, so the hosts could bring out the cheaper vintage and no one would know the difference.

At the marriage feast in Cana — which was attended by Jesus, his mother, and his disciples, plus many others — they ran out of wine near the end of the feast. In short, there were a lot of people there and they brought their thirsts with them. As we read, Jesus' mother knew Jesus could solve the problem, so she told the servants to do whatever Jesus asked. After a brief and mild rebuff of his mother for putting him in the position of having to solve the problem, Jesus told the servants to fill each of the six nearby water jugs to the top with water. Each one held 20 to 30 gallons. When they had done as Jesus requested, Jesus told them to draw some out and give it to the master of the banquet. We then read how the banquet master went to the bridegroom and asked him why he had saved the best wine until the end when the custom was to serve the best wine first. The banquet master did not know what Jesus had done, but the servants did, according to the biblical account.

Now let's be clear about what happened. Jesus turned between 120 to180 gallons of water into the finest and best wine available. That's a lot of wine, and it wasn't just grape juice. The Bible says wine, and people don't get merry (high) on grape juice — wine has an alcoholic content.

There's no indication Jesus drank any of the wine, but he was at a feast that went on for two or three days, and can anyone with a straight face believe he was there without laughing or sharing a humorous comment with some of the guests? In Ecclesiastes 10:19,

we read "A feast is made for laughter and wine makes life merry..."
These were fun occasions for the people, and anyone who attended
did so because they wanted to have a good time. We believe Jesus
had a good time, and obviously through his miracle he made it a
more merry time for many than it otherwise would have been. It
seems impossible to me that Jesus, with his wit and brilliant mind,
wouldn't have played an important part in the festive occasion. But
there's more about his sense of humor, much more.

Before going on, it is necessary to define a key word in describing the
humor of Jesus. That word is *irony*. The dictionary defines irony as "a
method of humorous or sarcastic expression in which the intended
use of the words is the direct opposite of their usual sense." I believe
we find in the Bible several instances where Jesus used this type of
humor. We find Jesus, in his wit and wisdom, often uses figures of
speech and comparisons that have an element of humor and irony
in them, although they are intended to make a serious point.

One of these instances occurs in Matthew 7:3-5 (also Luke 6:41),
where we read that Jesus is teaching about the dangers of judging
others. Here Jesus says in effect, "Why do you look at the speck
of sawdust in your brother's eye and fail to notice the log in your
own eye?" Jesus asks his listeners how they can possibly pay so
much attention to the faults of others while avoiding their own. The
idea of a log being in someone's eye is a humorous absurdity used
to make a powerful point. Jesus follows this statement with more
irony. In Matthew 7:6 he says, "Do not give dogs what is sacred; do
not throw your pearls to pigs..." Throwing pearls to swine and
giving valuable and sacred items to dogs again illustrates how Jesus
used absurdity to make critical arguments.

A similar instance of Jesus using a humorous exaggeration to
make an important point is found in Matthew 23:24, where he
is addressing the Pharisees and exposing their hypocrisy. Jesus
is upbraiding them for paying attention to some minor religious

duties while being oblivious to the more basic principles. To reinforce his point, Jesus says that the Pharisees, in their hypocrisy "strain out the gnats while they swallow a camel." Now, if one allows oneself to ponder trying to swallow a large, furry camel, humps and all, it should produce a smile. If you can visualize a Pharisee approaching a camel, which has that silly smile on its face and a penchant to spit on anyone who comes too close to their face, it gets even more humorous. Again, we see Jesus using irony to make a critical point.

Still another example of Jesus' irony is displayed in Matthew 19:24 (also Luke 18:25 and Mark 10:25), where we find Jesus addressing the rich young ruler, and teaching about the danger of great riches. He then says, "It is easier for a camel to go through the eye of a needle than for a rich man to enter the kingdom of heaven." Some translators believe the eye of the needle here refers to the doorway in the city gate for people to pass through when the large gates were not open. It really doesn't matter which Jesus meant for either is preposterous. For a large camel to get through a needle or a small doorway is impossible. That fact is reinforced by the disciples when they heard Jesus say this because their response was "Who then can be saved?" Jesus' response, of course, was that "all things are possible with God."

We see yet another example of irony from Jesus when he calls Andrew, Peter, James, and John to be his disciples (Mark 1:16-20, Matthew 4:18:22, and Luke 3:1-11). Jesus says, in effect, "Come with me and I will make you fishers of men." An interesting thought, with a touch of humor, but a profound statement with deep meaning for men whose profession was fishing. I'm sure that bit of humor helped attract the disciples to Jesus.

So, here we have at least four recorded instances of Jesus using irony in his dialog and teaching. Are these the only times he used this form of discourse? I doubt it very much, since so little of what Jesus said during his public ministry was recorded. It is totally logical to believe these instances reflect a pattern of discourse used by Jesus, and that, in turn, points to the fact he had a true sense of humor.

We have seen how Jesus made humorous comparisons and exaggerations in order to make a significant point in his teaching. Any good speaker or writer can appreciate the value of using such irony because it promotes retention of the information when it is related to something humorous or absurd. Jesus indeed was a masterful teacher. It is not hard to imagine, in the years after Jesus' ministry, that when his disciples got together they said, "Remember when Jesus compared the hypocrisy of the Pharisees to swallowing the gnat and camel? Or the speck and log in the eyes of the judgmental?" The humorous visual images conjured up by these figures of speech helped the disciples and all who heard them remember the points their Master Teacher wanted them to not forget.

Another occasion where we see the lighter side of Jesus is in the story of the Samaritan women at Jacob's well, as reported in John 4. After Jesus tells the woman that he can give her "living water," she says, in effect, "Give me this water." Jesus answers, "Go call your husband and come back here." Can't you just see the twinkle in Jesus' eye when he asks the woman to get her husband, knowing all along she has no husband? With a touch of humor, Jesus tests the woman. She passes the test when she responds that she has no husband. I can't help but believe Jesus was smiling when he then said to the woman, "You speak truthfully for you have had five husbands and the man you now have is not your husband." Jesus must have delighted in watching the woman's countenance as he told her about her past. Not only was Jesus a Jew talking to a Samaritan, which was contrary to practice, but he was proving to her he had supernatural power and could help her.

There are many ways Jesus could have addressed the woman at the well. He could have flat out told her he was the Christ and then proved it with some supernatural miracle. But instead he chose to ask her a question that allowed him to convince her he was special by telling her about her background. I believe that in the method Jesus chose, we see a glimpse of a lighter side and a sense of humor.

In the story of the woman caught in adultery and brought to Jesus by the Pharisees (John 8:3), we see a touch of humor in a serious situation where the religious leaders were setting a trap for Jesus. As you will recall, the Pharisees brought the woman to Jesus, saying she had been caught in adultery and according to Moses' Law she should be stoned to death. They then asked Jesus what he would do. At first, Jesus did not respond, rather he stooped down and wrote in the dirt with his finger. This act infuriated the Pharisees, who insisted he respond because they believed he would answer in such a way as to incriminate himself. After a bit of time, and further insistence on a response, Jesus rose up and said, "He among you who is without sin cast the first stone." With that, they all left. Then we see a bit of humor. Jesus says to the woman, "Where are they? Did no man condemn thee?" She answers, "No man, Lord." Then Jesus said, in effect, he didn't condemn her either, and that she should go on her way and sin no more.

In asking the question "Where are they?" Jesus showed a slight bit of humor. He knew the Pharisees had left and so did the woman. It was a rhetorical question. Again I believe, with a twinkle in his eye, Jesus asked a question he knew the answer to in order to make a critical point. Maybe it was humorous, maybe not, but at the least it was a brilliant handling of a tense situation.

Lastly, I believe we see a touch of humor in Jesus in his resurrected state when he meets two of his followers on the road to Emmaus. In Luke 24:13-32, Jesus draws near to the two disciples who are walking toward Emmaus and discussing the events of that momentous weekend. They had just heard the news the tomb Jesus had been placed in was empty, and some women who had gone to the tomb said some angels had told them Jesus was alive. Jesus hurries to catch up to the two men, and asks them what they are talking about. Jesus must have had a smile on his face as one of the men, named Cleophas, and his friend, talked about him and the events of that weekend, including the women's report of the empty tomb, and the angels reporting Jesus was alive.

Jesus explains to the two men all of the biblical references to himself and the resurrection. He then goes with them to eat. We read in the Bible that after he blessed the meal, he disappeared from the table just as the men were coming to the realization of who he was. I believe Jesus enjoyed his meeting with these men, and the way he revealed his identity. Maybe it was humorous, maybe not, but it was certainly an interesting way to deal with the situation.

Randy Alcorn sums things up well when he states, "Who is the most intelligent, creative, witty, and joyful human being in the universe? Jesus Christ. Whose laughter will be loudest and most contagious in the New Earth? Jesus Christ's (Alcorn 2004, 410).

One of the great Christian writers of the 20th century, Elton Trueblood sums up the issue of Jesus and humor by stating in his book, *The Humor of Christ* (Harper & Row, 1964), "If Christ laughed a great deal, as evidence shows, and if he is what he claimed to be, we cannot avoid the logical conclusion that there is laughter and gaiety in the heart of God (Trueblood, 1964, 32)." This is very true, but there is even more evidence than this. Let's take a look at the nature of humor itself. Is it good or bad? Is it something consistent with the nature of God? There's proof that indeed it is good and consistent with God's nature, as we shall soon see.

The Nature of Humor

If we take a closer look at the character of humor and the laughter it produces, we can obtain some clues as to whether it is good, bad, or neutral. This can give us further information about humor and laughter, and help us determine if they are characteristics likely to be associated with God. Logically we can say, if the nature of humor/laughter is bad or harmful, it is not a quality that would be associated with God, whose nature is good and perfect. On the contrary, if humor/laughter is basically good, healthy, and positive, then it could be a Godlike quality.

Before looking at some fascinating new scientific evidence on laughter, we should acknowledge that there are different types of laughter, and there is some question among experts about why we laugh, or at least what the internal mechanisms are in us that cause us to laugh. We tend to laugh under the following conditions:

A.) When a humorous word picture is painted (that we are able to visualize) or a funny picture or cartoon is viewed.

B.) When we're scared or nervous. This nervous laughter seems to relieve tension and help us overcome difficult situations.

C.) When something good happens to us. When we're happy and joyful, we tend to smile and laugh to express our good feelings.

D.) When we're tickled. We all seem to have sensitive spots on our bodies, that when tickled, cause us to laugh. This phenomenon is evident in babies almost from birth.

E.) When our minds are jerked. This aspect of laughter still puzzles the experts who study laughter and its physiological characteristics. Most jokes cause laughter by jerking our minds. The joke takes us down a particular, logical path and then the punch line suddenly takes us to another conclusion. The experts have found that the punch line of a joke leads to a release of energy in the brain. They speculate that when the brain is suddenly moved from a pending, logical conclusion to a far different, humorous end, the brain releases some energy, which results in laughter.

It is clear God created us with the capacity to laugh and that laughing is a pleasant experience. And scientists have recently made some exciting new discoveries about humor and laughter. But first, where did the word humor come from and what does it mean? According to the *Encyclopedia Americana* (1998, Vol.14), the word humor is Latin for liquid, fluid, or moisture. In medieval times, physicians believed a person's temperament was determined by their balance in their body of four bodily fluids, or humors. The four humors were yellow, black, blood, and phlegm. It was believed that the humors were generally in balance in most individuals. If, however, one of the humors came to predominate, it expressed itself in a particular behavior. If the yellow humor prevailed, the person was choleric, or of a bilious nature, showing a quick temper. If the black humor predominated, the person would be melancholy, sad, and depressed.

If blood prevailed, the person was sanguine, confident, and upbeat. If the humor phlegm predominated, the person was phlegmatic, indifferent, and apathetic.

According to the theory above, a person's basic temperament and character were determined by the balance of the humors. A person was normal and healthy if the humors were in good balance. If the humors got out of balance, it was thought a person needed correction. As far back as Plato and Aristotle, laughter was considered to be a corrective action that could help put the humors back in balance. Aristotle is reported to have said that laughter "is a bodily exercise precious to health." A person having an excess of one humor came to be known as a "humorist" and was in need of laughter. Over time, a person who was skilled in causing laughter, and thus able to cure one whose humors were out of balance, became known as a "humorist," and a person who told jokes and saw the funny side of life was said to have a "sense of humor."

Down through the ages, there has been a definite link between humor, laughter, and health. We read in the Bible in Proverbs 17:22, "A cheerful heart is good medicine, but a crushed spirit dries up the bones." Solomon understood that cheerfulness and humor made for good health. As we've already seen, the ancient Greeks saw a connection between laughter and the healing process, using laughter to "put the humors back in balance." They even went so far as to include a visit to The House of Comedians for patients in their healing centers.

Voltaire is reported to have said, "The art of medicine consists of keeping the patient amused while Mother Nature heals the disease." Thomas Sydenham, a 17th century physician said, "The arrival of a good clown exercises more beneficial influence upon the health of a town than twenty asses laden with drugs." William Thackeray, the English novelist, wrote in the 1800s that "a good laugh is sunshine in a house." In short, all through history there has been a recognized association between humor and health, but it is only in recent times, with our development of a scientific knowledge of human physiology, that we have come to know how and why laughter heals.

Some interesting events took place in the U.S. in the 1970s regarding laughter and healing. In 1971, Dr. Hunter Adams formed the Gesundheit Institute in Virginia to help apply the principles of laughter to healing. Dr. Hunter "Patch" Adams was convinced that laughter promoted healing, and while opposed by many medical people, he was intent on practicing his beliefs. Dr. Adam's work grew in importance and acceptance among medical authorities, however, and in 1998 Universal Pictures released a movie entitled *Patch Adams*, starring Robin Williams, which portrayed Dr. Adams and his work. The Gesundheit Institute prospers today in Arlington, Virginia and a major, new health facility is being constructed in West Virginia to further apply Dr. Adam's work. Anyone wishing to learn more about Dr. Adam's and his work can go to his Web site at: www.patchadams.org.

Later in the 1970s, noted journalist Norman Cousins was suffering from a crippling arthritic condition that medical science could not cure. Cousins decided to take matters into his own hands and apply laughter, large doses of vitamin C, and positive thinking to his condition. It worked, and Cousins, in part using old Marx Brothers and Candid Camera tapes, laughed himself back to health. He then wrote a best-selling book entitled *Anatomy of an Illness as Perceived by the Patient* (Bantam Books, 1981). The work of Dr. Adams and the case of Norman Cousins did much to popularize the use of humor and healing. Yet scientific research was about to add a good deal more.

So, we have historical statements and some observed results that support the relationship of humor and health, but is there hard scientific evidence about how this happens? Happily, there is. First, physiologists tell us that when a person laughs heartily, several physiological events take place: the diaphragm drops, the lungs expand, additional oxygen is inhaled, the heart is gently massaged, heart rate and blood pressure temporarily rise, oxygen surges through the bloodstream, and the person experiences a rush and feeling of contentment. A good laugh can also give one's abdomen, shoulders, back, and facial muscles a good workout. All human beings have experienced good feelings when laughing, but we now know because of more recent research that the "high" we get from laughter has an even deeper cause than just the physiological sources mentioned above.

Medical researchers had previously discovered there were "opiate receptors" in the body, but they didn't know of any opiate (a substance that quiets, soothes, and deadens pain) produced by the body. In 1975, Dr. Chou Hao Li was doing research on the pituitary gland at University of California Medical Center in San Francisco when he discovered a unique hormone secreted from the anterior section of the pituitary gland. He called it B-lipotropin. A year later, further discoveries at a laboratory in Aberdeen, Scotland helped identify and clarify the existence of a morphinelike substance produced internally. They called the substance enkephalin, which was contained within Dr. Li's hormone B-lipotropin. Dr. Li later named the opiate or morphinelike substance "Endorphin'" which means "morphine within." Endorphin has come to be a term covering different peptides secreted in the brain that have these morphinelike qualities. Subsequent research by Dr. Li and others has further uncovered properties in these endorphins that have led some to call it the body's miracle drug. Endorphins do some remarkable things in the body when released: they relieve pain, improve memory, enhance the immune system, unblock blood vessels, and have anti-aging properties. Endorphins also scurry around the body cleaning up free radicals, which many researchers link to cancer. No wonder some medical people call these endorphins the body's miracle drug. But what does this have to do with humor? In short, it has a whole lot to do with it.

When researchers naturally tried to find out what caused the excretion of these endorphins they discovered some interesting facts. They found that four activities specifically caused the pituitary to produce this miracle drug. The activities are: laughing, exercise, listening to soothing music, and hugging and making love. In brief, science found a direct link between laughing and these other activities, and health, healing, and longevity. So the connection between laughing and health and healing, observed from biblical times to the present, was now explained and confirmed. Surprised? I'm not. The concept had a good deal of validity, including biblical support, and research just confirmed a marvelous part of God's creation.

The research above also helps explain some other information we have known for a while. For example, we have known that individuals in happy marriages have longer life spans than those who are single. We know that comedians and musicians tend to have longer life spans than those in other professions. And we certainly know today that people who exercise regularly are healthier and live longer than those who don't. To reiterate, we knew all this before, but now we know the physiological mechanisms by which it is accomplished.

In researching material for this book, I came upon some anecdotal evidence of the above as it relates to comedians. In 1900, the average life span was 47 years. Around 1900, a group of America's greatest comedians was born. Here are those comedians, their age at death, and their life spans and their dates of birth and death: Jack Benny, 80 (1894-1974); Milton Berle, 96 (1908-2002); Jimmy Durante, 87 (1893-1980); George Burns, 100 (1896-1996); Groucho Marx, 87 (1890-1977); Red Skelton, 84 (1913-1997); Fibber McGee, 91 (1896-1988); Edgar Bergen, 75 (1903-1978); and lastly, the incomparable Bob Hope, 100 (1903-2003). This group of comedians outlived their contemporaries by an average of 40 years. Is this a coincidence? I don't think so. It seems consistent with the scientific evidence above that laughter is a healthy practice which promotes good health and longevity. By the way, all of the above comedians also incorporated music into their presentations, giving them another source of endorphin release.

Similar evidence is available for musicians, and of course, the medical profession has demonstrated the value of exercise to good health and longevity. So now we have scientific evidence that laughing, singing, loving, and exercise lead to good health and longevity. As someone said recently, "A hug, a joke, a song, and a workout a day keeps the doctor away. The apple is optional, except for members of the Washington State Apple Grower's Association."

Before going on, it's important to mention that the field of medical science is using the above information on humor in increasing measure. There is now a professional association called the American Association of Therapeutic Humor (AATH). For anyone interested, their Web site is www.aath.org. At the Duke Medical Center, an organization called the Carolina Health and Humor Association is at work using and researching humor and health. Many hospitals now have "humor carts" that can be used with patients, and the holistic medical movement has a strong emphasis on using humor for healing. See their Web site at www.holistic.online.com/humor_therapy. In addition, articles are appearing regularly in medical and nursing journals further pushing back the frontiers of our knowledge of the subject.

So what does this have to do with God laughing? It seems to me that the plethora of evidence linking humor and laughing to health, healing, and physical well-being links laughter to goodness and to God who is the epitome of goodness. Some may see this as a "stretch" of logic, but I don't think so, particularly in light of all the other evidence presented in this book. Can humor and laughter be harmful? Yes, I believe it can be, but that does not negate the overwhelmingly positive effects of it. More will be said about harmful humor later. For now, let's just say most good things in life can be distorted and misused, and humor is no different.

Reinhold Neibuhr said that "Laughter is the beginning of prayer — humor is a prelude to faith." Victor Borge, the musician/humorist, who by the way lived to be 91, has said, "Humor is the shortest distance between two people." Can anyone deny something this good, with the potential to heal and create good health, has come from God?

In James 1:17 we read, "Every good and perfect gift is from above coming down from the Father of Heavenly Lights, who does not change like shifting shadows." If humor is a "good gift," with the healing and other positive properties listed earlier in this chapter, then it is fair to assume it is a "good gift" from God. In I Corinthians 6:19, we are told that a Christian's body is "a temple of the Holy Spirit" and that God literally dwells in us through the Holy Spirit. The point will be made later in Chapter 5 that humor is a vital part of the personalities of numerous outstanding Christian leaders, and of course, we've already made a case for the fact that it was a part of the personality of Jesus. This being so, it seems logical humor is a characteristic that is consistent with the presence of God. It's a short step then to conclude this "good gift" is also a part of the make-up of God himself. I believe it is, and as a result, I firmly believe God has a sense of humor, and that he has a hearty laugh, too.

Humor in God's Creation

If God is the Creator of the universe, and if he has a sense of humor, it stands to reason his sense of humor might be reflected in what he created. To this writer, that fact is abundantly clear, if we but stop and look closely at God's handiwork around us. That fact was also abundantly clear to the eminent Christian clergyman George A. Buttrick. In a sermon he preached in the University Church at Harvard, Buttrick said, "No somber God could have made a bullfrog or a giraffe."

God's humor in creation was brought home to me in an incident that occurred a few years ago. My son and his wife, who love animals, sold their home intending to build a new one on land they had purchased. They bought some 26 acres with the intention of building a home for themselves and the numerous animals they owned. They hoped to one day have a place where children could come enjoy and learn about the animals. Already owning some llamas, emus, horses, dogs, and a monkey, they had a hard time finding a place to rent with their house pets, and they asked if they could temporarily stay with my wife and me. We consented with the proviso that the monkey be kept in our basement.

So my son and his wife moved in, and suddenly we had a dog and a monkey as house guests. I became great friends with the monkey, whose name was Shyla. We had some fun times with her. Shyla was tethered to a cage in the basement and could wander about in a limited area to entertain herself. Sometimes my son would bring her upstairs and play with her. Shyla would sit on our laps and pick at the hairs on our arms, as you often see monkeys do to each other at the zoo. She assumed the small moles we had were bugs that needed to be retrieved. At any rate, the monkey became a friend and we got along famously.

One day I was playing with the Shyla, and at one point I was face to face with her — not more than six inches away, looking straight at her — when a thought hit me in a forceful way. The thought was that if God had created a creature with such a funny face, he must have a sense of humor. I also had the thought that Shyla was probably looking back at me thinking exactly the same thing. That experience, and that thought, have given birth to this chapter.

I'm sure every reader, if asked to list some humorous and funny animals, could do so. Who hasn't gone to a zoo and laughed at the antics of the chimpanzees, the monkeys, or the south end of a baboon going north. The kangaroos, giraffes, elephants, and hippos can impress anyone with their rich diversity, and yes, the humor in God's creation.

The following are pictures of some of the animals God has created. If you look at them honestly, I believe you must entertain the hypothesis that the God who created them must have a sense of humor. Added to each picture are some words I felt the animals might wish to say to us, if they could communicate directly. So, does God have a sense of humor? Go through the next few pages. It is my contention you will, at the very least, entertain that thought.

Photo by Michael Turco - Used with permission.

You think *I'm* funny looking?

How do you like my Easter bonnet? I made it myself.

Please don't tell my brother and me to get off the couch.
We like it here.

Hi folks, I'm a sloth bear. It's really hard work
being as lazy as I am.

How do you folks like my beard?
The girls over there like it, too.

Please don't comment about my weight.
I'm a bit thin-skinned about that.

Please don't frighten us, or my girlfriend and I
will go into our shells.

Hi, I'm a giraffe. I'll tell you,
when we have sore throats, we have sore throats.

Contrary to what you think by looking at me,
I have never been incarcerated.

Hello, I'm a river hog. My ears and whiskers
give me my distinguished appearance.

He missed the tag! He missed the tag!
Can't these umpires get anything right?

SAN DIEGO ZOO

Hello, I'm a mandrill. I want you to know that
I am far smarter than I look.

Hello, I want you to know I didn't get my black eyes fighting.
I'm a lover, not a fighter.

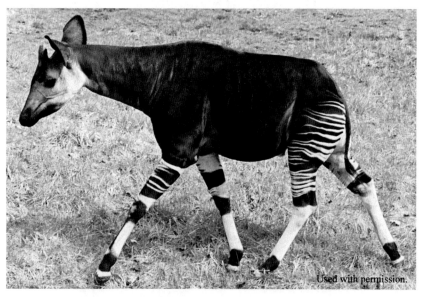

Hi, I'm an okapi. Do you like my zebra pants?
I wear them when I go to parties.

Hi folks, I'm Rocky. When I and my fellow shihtzus want to see
better we don't go to an optometrist, we go to our barbers.

Please don't comment about my ears. I like them
the way they are. I think they give me real class.

Hi, I'm Sadie, just an old hound dog.
I must say, these modern devices really bother me.

Hello, I'm a giant anteater.
If you have a problem with ants, give me a call.

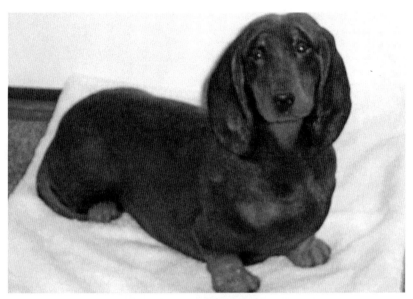

Please don't say I'm a half dog high and a dog and a half long.
I hear that all the time.

I'm a red panda. The giant pandas get all the attention, but I'm
really much more colorful and cuter. Aren't my ears neat?

Many sports teams call themselves tigers. That's because we represent toughness and strength. Are you a tiger fan?

Hi, I'm a Watusi steer from Africa. My horns are as prominent as my Texas longhorn relatives.

I'm a llama. God gave me a load limit. Put one pound more on my back than I'm programmed for and I won't move an inch.

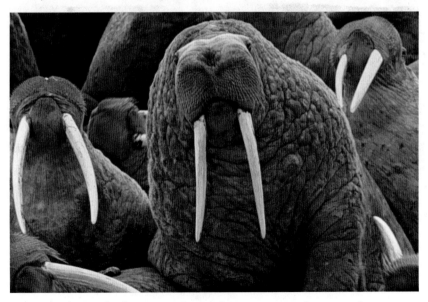

Please don't say anything about my two front teeth.
How's your smile?

I must tell you folks my eyesight isn't too great,
so don't stand in front of me.

It's cold up here, but our mom
takes good care of us.

Minden Pictures - Used with permission.

What was that you said about my intelligence?

So there you have it. Just a few of the wonderful animals God has created and gifted us with. They bring us pleasure, and yes, they bring us humor. These animals are but a very small representation of God's rich and wonderful creation. If we were to delve further into birds, insects, reptiles, and other categories of life, we would find countless other examples of humor in God's creation. And if God created these wonderful and complex creatures, you must admit, he must have a sense of humor.

The Creation story in Genesis indicates that God has given man a superior position in the order of things. He gave man the power to name, control and benefit from animals. If this is true, then it is logical to believe that God intended some of the animals for our enjoyment, too, and yes, some to cause us to laugh. If that is true, then it stands to reason that God himself has a sense of humor and indeed laughs.

Humor Among Christians

5

One way to gain evidence regarding humor and laughter is to look at the lives and character traits of outstanding Christians. If those who are mature Christians, and who are recognized as living godly lives, have a sense of humor, then it is logical to assume a sense of humor is a good characteristic. If they don't have it, or if they indicate it is not a good thing to have, we have proof that it is a negative element. I believe the evidence presented below demonstrates beyond a reasonable doubt that outstanding Christians, almost without exception, have a strong sense of humor.

Perhaps no Christian of our day is more revered than Billy Graham. If you have ever heard him preach, you know he has a sense of humor. I don't believe I've ever heard him preach in one of his crusades without using humor in his sermon. In one sermon, he said, "A Christian should live so that he would not be afraid to sell his parrot to the town gossip." While visiting New York, he commented to an associate as they tried to cross a busy street, "The only people in New York are the quick and the dead." Other examples of Dr. Graham's humor are found in the jokes in Appendix A at the back of this book. Suffice it to say, Billy Graham is a great Christian, and he has a wonderful sense of humor.

If you look at some of the popular TV preachers, such as Charles Stanley, Jerry Falwell, James Kennedy, Robert Schuller, and John Hagee, among others, every one of them uses humor from time to time, and every one can honestly be said to have a sense of humor. I have recently seen some of the old TV programs of the late Bishop Fulton Sheen. He was among the first of the great TV preachers, and he had a marvelous sense of humor. I believe part of his popularity was that people could sense in him a Christian joyfulness that was infectious.

One of the new, bright, young TV pastors is Joel Osteen. He is pastor of Lakewood Church in Houston, Texas. Lakewood Church has over 20,000 people in attendance every weekend. Osteen begins every sermon with a joke. The joke usually has nothing to do with the topic of the sermon; he simply tells a story to get the congregation to laugh together.

One of his recent stories was as follows:

> It seems God and Adam were having a conversation about Eve. Adam said, "God, why did you give Eve such a pretty face?" God replied, "So you'd love her, Adam." "Well, why did you give her such beautiful, blonde hair?" God again replied, "So you'd love her, Adam." "And why did you give her such a fine figure?" Again God said, "So you'd love her, Adam." Finally, Adam said, "Well, God why did you make her so dumb?" "I did that so she'd love you, Adam," God replied.

The congregation laughed, as they always do, and Osteen went on with his sermon. One might assume that the church that laughs together, grows and thrives together, based on Lakewood's experience.

Rick Warren is pastor of one of the largest and most influential megachurches in America, Saddleback Church in Southern California. I've heard him preach several times, and can personally testify he also has a keen sense of humor. His wife lovingly described him "as a real character" in a recent article.

One of the truly great servants of God is Brother Andrew, whose Open Doors Ministry has offices in 15 countries. Open Doors focuses on reaching and serving Christians in countries where the Christian church is persecuted. In a book written about his life, entitled *God's Smuggler*, which now has 10 million copies in print, Brother Andrew describes a most remarkable relationship and journey with God. At one point he writes, "God's faithfulness I was experiencing continually, and I was also finding out something about **his sense of humor**." (emphasis added, from *God's Smuggler*, Chosen Books, 2002, 73). In short, this man who walks close to God is constantly impressed with God's faithfulness, but also with God's sense of humor in dealing with him. My good friend, Dr. Doug Norwood, heads a mission ministry called Broken Jars. He also has a deep and close walk with God, and has a similar testimony regarding God's sense of humor in dealing with him.

Another great Christian of the 20th century, and a favorite of mine, was C.S. Lewis. He was a professor of English at Oxford University. Lewis converted to Christianity as an adult, at which time his literary skills were turned to the service of Christianity, and he became a strong force in defending and presenting the faith. His book *Mere Christianity* is perhaps the most important book on Christian apologetics ever written. His other books, such as *A Grief Observed, Surprised by Joy*, and a fictional work, *The Chronicles of Narnia*, are wonderful Christian works. The Disney Corporation in 2005 released a hit major motion picture based on *The Chronicles of Narnia* and the sequel was released in 2008. Another of his books is entitled *The Screwtape Letters*, in which we see a full-blown sense of humor as Lewis presents a satirical work about the devil and his work on earth. The book has sold millions of copies and has become a favorite of Christians all over the world. C.S. Lewis is another example of a great Christian with a marvelous sense of humor.

A writer by the name of Terry Lindvall has written a book about Lewis entitled *Surprised by Laughter — The Comic World of C.S. Lewis* (Thomas Nelson, 1996). Dr. Lindvall demonstrates beyond a doubt that C.S. Lewis had a wonderful and fully developed sense of humor.

One of the greatest evangelists and preachers of all time was Charles Spurgeon. This English clergyman, who lived in the latter half of the 19th century was the "Billy Graham" of his day. Spurgeon is the subject of a book entitled *Spurgeon on Leadership: Key Insights for Christian Leaders from The Prince of Preachers* (Kregel, Michigan 2003). The author of the book is Rev. Larry J. Michael, pastor of First Baptist Church of Sweetwater, Florida. Michael documents Spurgeon's sense of humor and writes that "Spurgeon was a man with a great sense of humor. He knew the value of laughter and mirth. He virtually took to heart the words in Proverbs 17:22 that 'A merry heart doeth good like a medicine.' " And if that were not enough evidence that humor and Christianity go together, it is reported that Martin Luther himself said, "If you're not allowed to laugh in heaven, I don't want to go there."

All of these outstanding Christian preachers value a sense of humor. This fact appears to confirm, beyond a doubt, that we can at least say laughing and having a sense of humor seems consistent with and complementary to being a good Christian. It also points to the fact that real Christians have a joy in their souls, which often manifests itself in humor and laughter. And if we can say that God's great people uniformly have a sense of humor, it also seems logical to say they are reflecting a characteristic consistent with and likely a direct part of the character of the God they serve and seek to emulate.

I have also heard someone say that laughter is the "music of the soul." I don't know if that is true. I suspect it is. But, if it is, the men listed above as servants of God sure know how to play "soul music."

Some of our great national leaders, who were Christians, also had a wonderful sense of humor. Abraham Lincoln, in the Lincoln-Douglas debates was berated by Steven Douglas at one point. Douglas accused Lincoln of being "two-faced." Lincoln's reply was, "Sir, if I had two faces do you think I'd wear this one?" It is also reported that Lincoln often would start his cabinet meetings with a joke. Some historians question whether Lincoln was a practicing Christian, however, in a visit to New York Avenue Presbyterian Church in Washington, D.C., I was told Lincoln often attended the church, and that he had made a commitment to join. He was scheduled to be received into membership but was killed by John Wilkes Booth just a week or so before he was to become a member.

American presidents George Bush numbers 41 and 43, both Christians, certainly have given evidence of having substantial senses of humor. Ronald Reagan had arguably one of the greatest senses of humors of any American president. When Billy Graham visited President Reagan after he had been shot, he told Graham "I forgot to duck." Just before being taken into the operating room, Reagan said, "I sure hope the doctors are Republicans."

Here are some of President Reagan's other famous quotes:

1. "Here's my strategy for the Cold War: We win, they lose."

2. "It has been said that politics is the world's second oldest profession. I have learned that it bears a striking resemblance to the first."

3. "I've laid down the law, though, to everyone from now on

about anything that happens: no matter what time it is, wake me, even if it's in the middle of a Cabinet meeting."

4. "Government's view of the economy could be summed up in a few short phrases: If it moves, tax it; if it keeps moving, regulate it; and if it stops moving, subsidize it."

5. "The nearest thing to eternal life we will ever see on this earth is a government program."

6. "Government is like a baby: an alimentary canal with a big appetite at one end and no sense of responsibility at the other."

7. "The trouble with our liberal friends is not that they're ignorant: it's just that they know so much that isn't so."

8. "I have wondered at times what the Ten Commandments would have looked like if Moses had run them through Congress."

Reagan's sense of humor served him and the nation well in so many difficult times.

Jimmy Carter, a self-declared born-again Christian, also showed a keen sense of humor. Carter, as have other presidents, had a problem with his brother. One day when talking to a group, Carter said about his brother, Billy, "I was going to involve Billy in government by putting the CIA and FBI together, but I didn't want him to head an agency he couldn't spell."

John F. Kennedy was reported to have a sharp wit also. When he was criticized for appointing his brother, Bobby, as attorney general, Kennedy said, "When I found out Bobby wanted to practice law, I decided he should get some experience." JFK was also fond of repeating a conversation he had with his good friend, Cardinal Spellman. Kennedy said he asked Spellman if the pope was really infallible. JFK indicated Spellman said, "I don't know, but he keeps calling me Spillman."

Winston Churchill, the great World War II leader of Great Britain who had American citizenship, claimed the Christian faith. He certainly is historically considered to be one of the world's great leaders, and he had a marvelous sense of humor. One time, Churchill was having a discussion with Lady Astor in the House of Lords, and she became exasperated with Churchill, finally saying to him, "Sir, if you were my husband, I'd put poison in your coffee!" Upon hearing this Churchill replied, "Madam, if I were your husband, I would gladly drink it." On another occasion, Churchill was talking about his political opponent, Clement Atlee, and he said, "Atlee is a very humble man with a great deal to be humble about."

Someone once said, "Laughter is God's hand on the shoulder of a troubled world." Comments like this capture the importance and character of laughter, and it is uniformly considered good and positive. Most great leaders and speakers have learned that humor can put people at ease, bind a group together, and smooth over differences. Can any element with those characteristics be bad? I don't think so. Humor not only can promote physical healing but it can promote psychological and social harmony as well. It's just plain hard to dislike someone with whom you're sharing a laugh. Such an element — with a potential for such good — could only come from and be consistent with the nature of God.

Humor in the Church

There is a good deal of humor in the Christian church itself. Having attended different churches, I am amazed to see people in conversations after church frequently smiling and sharing humorous thoughts together. At one church I attended, a group of men would, after church, get together to share some of the best stories they had heard that week. Humor was natural at church, and laughing was part of the ethos. Again, while this doesn't in and of itself prove that God laughs, it does say that humor and laughter are a natural part of a Christian gathering and therefore more likely to be good, wholesome, and a part of the character of God.

Often, I will get humorous stories from Christian friends, usually over the Internet. There is a pastor in Grand Rapids, Michigan who for years sent out a humorous story every Friday to a list of his friends and fellow pastors. Most Christians are aware of the lists of "bulletin bloopers" that are often passed around. One day, I received the following list of bloopers from a member of our church, who had sent it to everyone on the church e-mail list.

The following are actual statements that appeared in church bulletins:

1. The Scouts are saving aluminum cans, bottles, and other items to be recycled. Proceeds will be used to cripple children.

2. The Ladies Bible Study will be held Thursday morning at 10. All ladies are invited to lunch in the Fellowship Hall after the B.S. is done.

3. The pastor would appreciate it if the ladies of the congregation would lend him their electric girdles for the pancake breakfast next Sunday morning.

4. The Low Self Esteem Support Group will meet Thursday at 7:00 PM. Please use the back door.

5. The pastor will preach his farewell message, after which the choir will sing, "Break Forth into Joy."

6. A songfest was hell at the Methodist church Wednesday.

7. Remember in prayer the many who are sick of our church and community.

8. The eighth-graders will be presenting Shakespeare's Hamlet in the church basement Friday at 7 PM. The congregation is invited to attend this tragedy.

9. Thursday night potluck dinner with medication to follow.

10. The rosebud on the altar this morning is to announce the birth of David, the sin of the Rev. and Mrs. Adams.

11. Tuesday at 4 PM there will be an ice cream social. All ladies giving milk will please come early.

12. A bean supper will be held Tuesday evening in the church hall. Music will follow.

13. At the evening service tonight, the sermon topic will be "What is Hell?" Come early and listen to the choir practice.

14. Weight Watchers will meet at 7 PM at the Presbyterian Church. Please use the large double doors at the side entrance.

15. Our next song is "Angels We Have Heard Get High."

16. Don't let worry kill you, let the church help.

17. For those who have children and don't know it, we have a nursery downstairs.

18. This being Easter Sunday, we will ask Mrs. Lewis to come forward and lay an egg on the altar.

19. The senior choir invites any member of the congregation who enjoys sinning to join the choir.

20. Eight new choir robes are currently needed, due to the addition of several new members and the deterioration of some older ones.

Now, as God looks down on his church and sees bloopers like these, can you honestly believe he doesn't laugh? I believe he does!

There is a whole genre of jokes that has grown around entrance into heaven. These jokes usually involve someone approaching heaven, meeting Saint Peter at the gate, and asking to enter. I must confess that some of these jokes go over the line, are theologically incorrect, and may be told by non-believers to poke fun of those of faith, but many are very funny and theologically correct. Below are a few illustrations of the latter type.

1. A man approached Peter at the gate to heaven and said he'd like to enter. Peter said he could enter if he could get 100 points through good works on earth. The man said that he had been married to the same woman for 50 years and had never cheated on her. Peter said, "That's fine, that earns you 1 point." The man said he tithed all of his life. Peter said, "That's good, you get 1 more point." Then the man said he had a restaurant and gave the extra food to the poor, feeding many hungry people in his life. Peter said, "That's very good, you get two points for that." The man became frustrated with the few points he was getting and said, "Is that all the points I get? At this rate it'll take the grace of God to get me into heaven." Whereupon Peter said, "Bingo, you said the magic words. That earns you 100 points. Come on in!"

2. Saint Peter was giving a tour of heaven to some new arrivals. They heard singing as they neared a large building, and as they were about to pass by it, Saint Peter told the group not to talk or make any noise as they passed. Once by the building one of the new arrivals asked why they had to be quiet while passing. Saint Peter said, "Oh, the Baptists are in that building and they think they're the only ones up here."

3. Three men arrived at the Pearly Gates. Saint Peter asked the first where he was from and he said, "Chicago." Saint Peter said,

"You can go to hell." Saint Peter asked the second where he was from and he said, "Los Angeles." St. Peter said to him, "You to can go to hell." The third fellow didn't even wait for St. Peter's question. He said, "Saint Peter, I'm from Texas. Do I go to hell too?" Saint Peter shook his head and said, "No, you can enter heaven. Being from Texas, you've already been to hell."

Another genre of humor in the Christian church is stories of little children as they learn their faith and often get things somewhat mixed up. Below are some examples:

1. A little boy came downstairs and said to his dad, "Father, is it true man was created from dust?" His father said, "Yes, son, Adam was created from dust." The son then asked, "Father, is it true that we return to dust after we die?" His father again said, "Yes, why do you ask?" "Well," said the little boy, "I was just upstairs and I looked under my bed and there's someone up there either coming or going."

The following is a list of similar stories currently traveling about the Internet.

2. A little boy was in church for the first time and he was watching the ushers take up the collection. As the plate neared them, he piped up so everyone could hear, "Don't pay for me, Daddy, I'm under five."

3. A little boy was attending his first wedding. After the service, his cousin asked him, "How many women can a man marry?" "Sixteen," the boy replied. "How do you know that?" "It's easy," the little boy said. "You just have to add them up. Like the pastor said, four better, four worse, four richer, and four poorer."

4. After church one Sunday, a young boy announced to his parents he had decided to be a minister when he grew up. His

mother said, "That's okay with us, but what made you decide to become a pastor?" "Well," said the little boy, "If I have to go to church every Sunday, I figure it would be more fun to stand up front and yell rather than have to sit and listen."

5. A boy was watching his father, a pastor, write a sermon. "How do you know what to say?" he asked. "Why, God tells me," answered his father. "Oh, then why do you keep crossing things out?"

6. A little girl became restless as the preacher's sermon dragged on and on. Finally, she leaned over to her mother and said, "Mommy, if we give him the money now, will he let us go?"

7. After a christening of his baby brother in church, little Johnny sobbed all the way home in the back seat of the car. His father asked him three times what was wrong. Finally, the boy replied, "The pastor said he wanted all children to be brought up in a Christian home, and I want to stay with you guys."

8. Terri asked her Sunday school class to draw pictures of their favorite Bible stories. She was puzzled by Kyle's picture, which showed four people on an airplane, so she asked which story it was meant to represent. "The flight to Egypt," said Kyle. "I see," said Terri, "and that must be Mary, Joseph, and the baby Jesus. But who is the fourth person?" "Oh", said Kyle, "that's Pontius, the pilot."

9. The Sunday school teacher asked directly, "Now, Johnny, tell me frankly, do you say prayers before eating?" "Oh, no sir. I don't have to, my mother's a good cook."

10. A college drama group presented a play in which one character would stand on a trap door and announce, "I descend into hell!" A stagehand below would then pull a rope, the trap

door would open, and the character would plunge through. The play was well received, but one day, the actor who went through the trap door became ill, and a very much overweight actor took his place. When the new actor announced, "I descend into hell!" the stagehand pulled the rope and the actor became hopelessly stuck. No amount of tugging on the rope could make him descend. A little boy sitting in the balcony jumped up and yelled, "Hallelujah! Hell is full!"

Yes, the Christian church is full of humor. When I went on the Internet recently and punched in the words "Christian humor" on the Goggle search engine, I came up with over a million items. Clearly, there are numerous Web pages containing Christian humor. I found a "Fellowship of Merry Christians" that one can join, with a newsletter called *The Joyful Newsletter*. I found pastors and churches that regularly collect and post humorous items. And there are books like Cal and Rose Samara's series on Holy Hilarity published by WaterBrook Press and dedicated to promoting humor among Christians.

There is also a growing group of Christian comedians, who not only make people laugh, but who bring God's plan of salvation to people. Ken Davis is an example of an ordained minister who is an outstanding comedian. He could easily make millions in the secular comedy world, but he dedicates his talent to God instead. Geraldine Ragan is a ventriloquist of great talent. She and her dummy form the Geraldine and Ricky duo. They have kept Christians laughing from coast to coast, and have presented the Gospel to children and adults alike. Mark Lowry is another Christian comedian who sings and tells jokes. He is well-known from his appearances on the Bill Gaither programs. There are other Christian comedians, such as Rod Allison, Tim Hawkins, Michael Joiner, Jeff Allen, Dennis Swanberg, Chonda Pierce, Vyck Cooley, who are part of a growing list. There is even a Christian Comedy Association which has annual conventions. (Their Web site is www.christiancomedyassociation.

com.) With this much comedy among Christians, can anyone honestly say it isn't a wholesome, positive element?

No one can come away from the body of humor shared by Christians without concluding joy and humor are very much parts of the Christian church. I believe that this is good and wholesome, and a reflection of the internal joy that all true Christians experience. That being the case, it is logical to conclude this characteristic is a reflection of the nature of our God. It is then a short, logical step to conclude that God laughs.

Humor in America

There are two facts I believe are indisputable, and which further add to the proof that God and humor are linked. First, America as a nation has a Christian foundation. And second, America has the richest history of comedy and humor of any nation in the world. Is this a coincidence? I don't think so.

There's a debate going on in the U.S. today about whether we are or are not a Christian nation. This is not the place to debate that issue except to say the evidence for the historical Christian roots of our country is vast. Our history books chronicle the settlement of the colonies, in large part, by Christians seeking religious freedom. Our founding documents, such as the Mayflower Compact and the Declaration of Independence, reflect the religious character of our founding fathers. Of the 55 signers of the Declaration of Independence, 52 were Christians and about half were clergymen.

As late as 1892, the U.S. Supreme Court declared in the Trinity Decision that the U.S. was a Christian nation. In short, while we have strayed from our heritage to a large extent and are more diverse now, it doesn't change the fact that our foundation is in the

Christian tradition. Our history and our values have been stamped rather firmly with that fact. In spite of the current "culture war," and the efforts of some groups like the American Civil Liberties Union (ACLU) and Americans United for Separation of Church and State to create a secular America, there can be little doubt that our founders were primarily Christians, and they founded this nation on Judeo-Christian principles.

One of the most astute observers of the U.S. was a French nobleman who came to these shores in the 1830s. Alexis de Tocqueville spent years crisscrossing the country, talking to people and trying to find out what made this "new" democracy tick. He wrote the classic book entitled *Democracy in America* (Bantam Classics, 2000). The book is required reading in most college American history classes. In his book, de Tocqueville says, "In the United States the sovereign authority is religious . . . there is no country in the whole world in which the Christian religion retains a greater influence over the souls of men than in America . . . its (Christianity) influence is most powerfully felt over the most enlightened and free nation of the earth (from *Democracy in America*, de Tocqueville, 2000, 350-351)."

The point is that the Christian foundations of America laid a rich groundwork from which a body of humor arose. Arguably, America has produced the richest reservoir of humor the world has ever known. Even though some of our religious forefathers were Calvinists and fundamentalists, who were suspicious of humor because some thought it too close to deviltry, the nation accepted, endorsed, and encouraged humor. While some may feel the argument farfetched, I believe our historical religious roots, the freedom it produced, and the joy of the faith that came from belief were factors in our nation developing such a rich foundation of humor. One can, I believe, honestly say humor is part of the American character. And with that, let's briefly examine the history of humor in the U.S.

Perhaps the first American comedic writer was Ben Franklin. Most historians categorize Franklin as a deist, though he often attended the Presbyterian Church in Philadelphia. Franklin published his classic, *Poor Richard's Almanac*, in the 18th century. The book is filled with aphorisms and proverbs, many of which reflect Franklin's keen sense of humor. Almanacs were a source of humor as the printing press increased the availability of reading material. And as the population became more educated, there was a greater demand for such material. Between1830 and 1860, the comic almanacs became very popular in the U.S. In 1833, we also saw the beginning of joke books, with the publication of the Joe Miller joke books.

In 1835, Samuel Clemens was born. He would write under the name of Mark Twain and become one of America's favorite humorists. His first book was *The Celebrated Jumping Frog of Calaveras County*, published in 1867. Just a few years later, in 1879, another of America's great humorists was born. Will Rogers entered the world and would entertain Americans for years with his humorous observations of American life, with a special focus on our political foibles. From its early days, our country had its share of stage shows, side shows, circuses, and clowns. But much of our comic heritage was incubated in a vigorous vaudeville institution, which flourished in the U.S. between the 1870s and 1920s. With the development of the media — the radio first, then movies, and then television — comedy was given a national audience and it really took off.

A number of comedians and comediennes born around the turn of the century were to keep America laughing for a century. Many of them polished their talents in vaudeville shows. They were to play a major role in developing and enhancing America's "funny-bone." They were people like W.C. Fields (1880), Groucho Marx (1890), Jimmy Durante (1893), Jack Benny (1894), Fibber McGee (1896) and his wife and partner, Molly (1899), George Burns (1896), Milton Berle (1908), Lucille Ball (1911), Red Skelton (1913), and Phyllis Diller (1917). Four other comedians born in foreign countries at this time would come to American and do most of their professional work here. They were Bob Hope, born in England in 1903 (Hope said he came to America when he found out he couldn't be King of England); Charlie Chaplin, born in England in 1889; Stan Laurel, of Laurel and Hardy, born in England in 1890; and Victor Borge, born in Denmark in 1909.

Charlie Chaplin and his "Little Tramp" character captured America's heart during the silent movie days and made Chaplin a worldwide success. Unfortunately, Chaplin got into trouble with our government over tax evasion and his leftist political views, and was ultimately denied readmission to the U.S. after he made a trip to Europe. Chaplin would spend his remaining days in Switzerland, but his contribution to American humor has been lasting.

A humorous event occurred while Chaplin was living in Europe. Every year, an annual Chaplin look-a-like contest was held in Monaco. One year, when Chaplin was there incognito, he decided to enter the contest. To his chagrin, he came in third.

As our movie industry developed, numerous comedians took advantage of it. Laurel and Hardy, Abbott and Costello, the Three Stooges, the Marx Brothers, and others became American and worldwide favorites as our movies spread to foreign lands.

On the radio, people were listening to Fibber McGee and Molly, just waiting for them to open their famous closet door. They were followed on the airways by George Burns and Gracie Allen, Amos and Andy, Edgar Bergen and Charlie McCarthy, who made listening to their radio programs a comedic feast.

In the 1930s and 1940s our humor took to the highways with a new type of advertising in the form of Burma Shave signs. These signs were placed in a sequence along well-traveled highways, spaced so one could read them one at a time in order. The signs had a humorous message, often related to driving, and would always end with the sign of the sponsor, Burma Shave, the maker of a shaving cream. Drivers and their passengers would look for these entertaining signs as they drove the highways of America.

Here are some of the Burma Shave sign sequences:

1. Car in ditch
2. Driver in tree
3. The moon was full
4. So was he
5. Burma Shave

1. Passing school zone
2. Take it slow
3. Let our little
4. Shavers grow
5. Burma Shave

1. At intersection
2. Look each way
3. A harp sounds nice
4. But it's hard to play
5. Burma Shave

1. A guy who drives
2. A car wide open
3. Is not thinkin'
4. He's just hopin'
5. Burma Shave

1. Around the curve
2. Lickety split
3. It's a beautiful car
4. Wasn't it?
5. Burma Shave

1. The midnight ride
2. Of Paul for beer
3. Led to a warmer
4. Hemisphere
5. Burma Shave

1. Brother speeder
2. Let's rehearse
3. All together
4. Good morning nurse
5. Burma Shave

1. Drove too long
2. Driver snoozing
3. What happened next
4. Is not amusing
5. Burma Shave

The Burma Shave signs presaged the humor that pervades much of today's advertising. Most of us will agree television contains some hilarious advertisements. Advertisers have come to realize that if they can make people laugh at their ads, they will build a positive relationship to their product and get people to talk with others about them, further stretching the impact of the ad.

Milton Berle led the charge of humor onto TV and opened the door to a new age of comedy, brought into our living rooms first in black and white and then in living color. *I Love Lucy, The Honeymooners, The Dick Van Dyke Show,* and *The Mary Tyler Moore Show* became national treasures and had worldwide audiences. Bob Hope, Jack Benny, Red Skelton, Danny Kaye, Red Buttons, Victor Borge, Dean Martin and Jerry Lewis, and a host of others soon followed and kept America laughing through recessions, wars, and troubled times. Jokes told on TV would spread across the nation almost overnight as people passed them on around the water cooler at work.

Our national "funny bone" runs deep and broad, and encompasses a wide variety of humor. From sitcoms to individual jokes, from ethnic humor to jokes about lawyers and politicians, from satire to cartoons, from gags and caricatures to riddles and epigrams, from April Fool jokes to riddles and funny stories, from late night talk shows to comedy clubs, from the funny pages to comic books, you name it, and if people laugh at it, we have it in America in abundance.

In the mid-1950s a multi-talented Dave Garroway pioneered the late night talk show filled with humor. Steve Allen followed Garroway and *The Tonight Show* became a hit and a fixture in America. Jack Paar took over in the late 1950s and early 1960s. He gave way to the incomparable Johnny Carson, who developed the show even further and would put America to bed laughing for nearly 30 years. Now Jay Leno and David Letterman do *The Tonight Show* and *The Late Show* respectively. They keep us laughing at ourselves and feed our national sense of humor. And on Saturday nights, we've had *Saturday Night Live* to hold us over to Monday when the late shows return.

In 1968, a TV show came along that was to keep America smiling for years. Because of its format, it would create a springboard for the careers of a host of comedians who would play regular or cameo parts on the show. The show was the *Rowan and Martin's Laugh-In*. It was a hit from the beginning because of its laugh-a-minute pace. They did 124 shows over a five-year period and people are still laughing at them today on tape and video disc.

Many of our comedians have had worldwide careers because American movies and TV programs have worldwide distribution. And because of the predominance of the English language around the world, our comedians literally have a worldwide impact. For all of these reasons, America has become the humor center of the world.

Some of our comedians have even developed formulas for their comedy. Consider the following stars:

1. Rodney Dangerfield made a career out of saying "I get no respect" and putting himself down. For example, he said, "My psychiatrist said I was crazy, so I asked him if I could get a second opinion. He said, 'Yes, you're ugly, too.' "

2. Jeff Foxworthy has made a career out of saying, "you're a redneck if . . ." For example, "You're a redneck if you wear white socks and drink Blue Ribbon beer," or "You're a redneck if you go lookin' for girls at Wal-Mart."

3. Phyllis Diller made a career out of getting people to laugh with her about how homely she was. She once said, "I'm so homely, a peeping tom asked me to pull my shade down."

Jack Benny made a fortune playing a stingy person and playing the violin badly, Milton Berle on admitting he stole others' jokes, Don Rickles on putting people down. Foster Brooks was perhaps the very best at playing a drunk, though numerous comedians have used that comedic genre. One time, Brooks was asked what the key was to playing a successful drunk and he made an interesting comment. He said, to play a drunk realistically, you had to play a person who is drunk but trying to appear sober and can't — an insight that led to his remarkable success.

Edgar Bergen was perhaps the most successful ventriloquist, with his pals Charlie McCarthy and Mortimer Snerd. Red Skelton had a stable of characters, such as the Punch Drunk Fighter, Willie Lumplump, Freddy the Freeloader, Deadeye, and San Fernando Red.

As a baseball fan, I have been intrigued about how America's sense of humor has even infiltrated major league baseball. Two baseball greats stand out above many others as making Americans laugh. It is also appropriate to the arguments made in this chapter, regarding humor and American character, that both men are known as "Yankees." I'm referring, of course, to Casey Stengel and Yogi Berra.

Casey Stengel had a distinguished playing career in the National League but will go down in baseball history for managing the New York Yankees to ten American League pennants and five straight World Championships. Yogi Berra played on some of those Yankees teams and was one of the best catchers ever to play the game, being selected to the All-Star team 15 times. Later, he managed the Yankees himself. What is unique, however, is the impact these men had on our English language and our sense of humor. Both men had a way of saying things and using our language that made us think and laugh like few others have. Some sportswriters came to call much of what Casey Stengel said "Stengelese." As an example, here are ten statements made by Casey Stengel that are still widely quoted:

1. "All right, everyone, line up alphabetically according to your height."

2. "Good pitching will always stop good hitting and vice-versa."

3. "Don't cut my throat, I may want to do that later myself."

4. "I don't know if he throws a spitball or not, but he sure spits on the ball a lot."

5. "I don't like them fellows who drive in two runs and let in three."

6. "I got players with bad watches — they can't tell midnight from noon."

7. "I was such a dangerous hitter I even got intentional walks during batting practice."

8. "If you're so smart, let's see you get out of the Army."

9. "Mr., that boy couldn't hit the ground if he fell out of an airplane."

10. "It's wonderful to meet so many friends I didn't used to like."

Reporters loved to interview Stengel because they frequently got a comment in "Stengelese" that would spice up a story. People often wondered whether Stengel was dumb or a humorist. Yogi Berra said about Stengel, "He could fool you. When Casey Stengel wanted to make sense he could, but he usually preferred to make you laugh." Stengel's widow has said Casey was a brilliant man. It seems he liked to make people laugh. I doubt a man of average intelligence could manage a major league baseball team to ten pennants and five straight world championships.

Yogi Berra gained the reputation for saying things that seemed on the surface to be dumb, but at times also seemed to have a deeper meaning. Here are some famous statements from Yogi that are still often used and laughed at by Americans.

1. "You can observe a lot by just watching."

2. "It ain't the heat, it's the humility."

3. "This is like déjà vu all over again."

4. "Baseball is 90% mental. The other half is physical."

5. "Slump? I ain't in a slump, I just ain't hitting."
6. "It ain't over till it's over."
7. "I made a wrong mistake."
8. "I knew I was going to take the wrong train, so I left early."
9. "You should go to other people's funerals; otherwise they won't come to yours."
10. "If you come to a fork in the road, take it."
11. "Nobody goes there anymore, it's too crowded."

Are these statements dumb? Funny? Profound? I believe the jury may still be out, but what can't be denied is that Yogi Berra has caused a lot of people to laugh and think. When Casey Stengel was asked whether Yogi was dumb he said, "I don't know, but I know he's a multimillionaire, has a beautiful wife, lives in a mansion, plays golf with celebrities, and gets into country clubs I can't get into." Stengel said what most people believe, and that is Berra has turned himself into an American institution, has things he has said often repeated in speech and writing, has an honorary doctorate in humanities, and makes millions. While this is being written, Berra is appearing in a popular TV commercial for the AFLAC Insurance Company. He's sitting in a barbershop, talking to a man in the next chair about liability insurance, and Berra says to the fellow that if something were to happen to him, he would "get cash, which is just as good as money." Everyone in the barbershop, including the AFLAC duck, have stunned looks on their faces, wondering what they just heard. Some would say Berra is dumb — like a fox on his way to the bank.

Whatever the case is about Casey Stengel and Yogi Berra, it cannot be denied that they are loved and revered by Americans, they have brought us many laughs, and they have affected our language. This couldn't have happened in a country that didn't have a sense of humor.

Cartoons and funny pages in our newspapers play a large role in

American humor as well. During the Depression, the mayor of New York City, Fiorello La Guardia, would read the comic pages to the children of New York over the radio to keep their spirits up and sense of humor alive.

In 1948, a cartoonist sold his first comic strip to the *Saturday Evening Post*. This was a major step in the career of the most popular cartoonist in the history of the world, namely, Charles Schultz. His strip, entitled *Peanuts*, would ultimately appear in 2,600 papers and publications and earn Schutlz over $55 million before his death in 2000. Peanuts still appears in syndication and led to an industry built around the strip, and characters such as Snoopy, Lucy, Linus, etc. As a former catcher, one of my favorite Peanuts cartoons is the following:

Used with permission of United Media.

Charles Schultz was influenced by the Bible, and his comic strip, while humorous, also pointed out basic moral principles. This gave rise to a book entitled *The Gospel According to Peanuts* by Robert Short.

Another cartoonist who is very popular today is a Christian and his values and faith often pop up in his *B.C.* comic strip. Johnny Hart is the cartoonist and a sample of his strip is on the following page. Unfortunately Johnny Hart died while this book was being written, however, his comic strip will continue in syndication, as does *Peanuts*.

One of my favorite cartoonists is Randy Glasbergen. He has clean and funny strips that can be seen in many publications and on his Web site at: www.glasbergen.com. His strip *The Better Half* is in many papers and examines the vicissitudes of married life. Below are two of Glasbergen's cartoons.

"There was a tunnel and a bright white light
and a souvenir shop! I brought back
T-shirts for the kids!"

© 1997 Randy Glasbergen. www.glasbergen.com

"I'm getting a message from your dear,
departed wife. She says it's okay if
you leave the seat up now."

Professional comedians, cartoonists, and humorists certainly reign
supreme in the U.S., but there is plenty of humor in everyday life that
we the common people create, pick up, and share with each other as
well. Below is a list of actual signs found on American businesses.
The list has been passed around the Internet and was forwarded to
the me by a pastor who enjoys humor.

1. Sign over a gynecologist's office:
   "Dr. Jones, at your cervix."
2. On a plumber's truck:
   "We repair what your husband fixed."
3. On a plumber's truck:
   "Don't sleep with a drip. Call your plumber."
4. At a tire shop:
   "Invite us to your next blowout."
5. On a plastic surgeon's office door:
   "Hello. Can we pick your nose?"
6. On a proctologist's door:
   "To expedite your visit please back in."
7. On a maternity room door:
   "Push. Push. Push."

8. At an optometrist's office:
   "If you don't see what you're looking for, you came to the right place."
9. On an electrician's truck:
   "Let us remove your shorts."
10. On a pizza shop:
    "Seven days without pizza makes one weak."
11. On a taxidermist's window:
    "We really know our stuff."
12. In a podiatrist's office:
    "Time wounds all heels."
13. Outside a muffler shop:
    "No appointment needed. We hear you coming."
14. At a car dealership:
    "The best way to get back on your feet is to miss a car payment."
15. In a veterinarian's waiting room:
    "Be back in 5 minutes. Sit! Stay!"
16. In the front yard of a funeral home:
    "Drive carefully. We'll wait."
17. At a propane filling station:
    "Tank heaven for little grills."
18. At a radiator shop in Chicago:
    "The best place to take a leak."
19. In a restaurant window:
    "Don't stand there and be hungry. Come in and get fed up."
20. On a septic tank truck:
    "We're #1 in the #2 business."

Could a nation without a sense of humor produce signs like these? I seriously doubt it.

One very important part of American culture is country and western music. These songs about life are both serious and at times comical. The following are some of the actual titles of country and western songs over the years.

1. "I've Got Four on yhe Floor and a Fifth Under the Seat"
2. "Jesus, Drop Kick Me through the Goal Posts of Life"
3. "I'm Having Day Dreams about Night Things in ihe Middle of the Afternoon"
4. "Don't All the Girls Get Prettier at Closing Time?"
5. "Flushed from the Bathroom of Your Heart"
6. "You're the Hangnail of My Life and I Can't Bite You Out"
7. "King Kong Is a Monkey Compared to My Love for You"
8. "When I Reached for Her Body She Reached for My Soul"
9. "Don't Come Home a Drinkin' with Lovin' on Your Mind"
10. "If I Said You Had a Beautiful Body, Would You Hold It Against Me?"
11. "You Can't Have Your Kate and Edith, Too"
12. "I'm Ruth-less"
14. "Let's Fall to Pieces Together before We Fall Apart"
15. "I Don't Want Your Body If Your Hearts Not in It"
16. "How Can I Miss You If You Won't Leave?"

Can anyone deny that a country that produces signs, songs, and writing like the above has a rich and fully developed sense of humor? I think not.

America has also used humor to get the nation through tough times. During World War II, a creature named Kilroy appeared (see next page.) began appearing all over the country, particularly where our armed forces went. The phrase "Kilroy was here" began to appear all over, bringing a laugh to all who saw it. Kilroy would appear on munitions used by the military, on buildings and fences, on stationary, and in many unexpected places. Kilroy elicited laughs during a very difficult period in American history. Our American sense of humor again played a helpful role.

Kilroy Was Here

To reiterate the basic premise of this chapter, because the U.S. was founded on Christian principles and values, it is my contention that we have developed the greatest body of humor the world has ever known. No nation, even other Western nations from which the U.S. was born, has produced the humor we have. Why is this so? First, I believe the U.S., as Alexis de Tocqueville pointed out above, was the most Christian of any nation in history. Many other nations in history were "Christian," however, they invariably had state churches, which limited people's religious freedom to a specific kind of Christianity, and often persecuted Christians who disagreed with the state religion. America, because of its broader Christian values committed itself to far fuller religious freedom.

We have religious freedom in this country largely because our nation's founders accepted the Christian premise that people cannot and should not be forced to become believers. They felt a coerced faith had little value. The Christian faith teaches that God has given each of us the freedom to accept or reject him (free agency in theological terms). This is based on the premise that love not freely given has no value. God wants us to love him, the argument goes, but for that love to have value, it must be given without force or pressure. The choice to reject God, therefore, must be an option for the love to have real meaning. It is this writer's contention that this belief — the necessity for people to have freedom of choice in religion — was the cornerstone upon which America built its commitment to freedom of religion as a constitutional foundation. We have religious freedom because we believe people must freely choose to believe and cannot be coerced to do so

We also have religious freedom because our forefathers realized early on that the U.S. would have various forms of Christianity and even other religions. They very much wanted to avoid the state churches of Europe and the forced religiosity they had experienced. The net result of all this is that the U.S. developed a Bill of Rights whose first article guaranteed Americans the freedom of religion and speech. This foundation of freedom provided the fertile ground upon which our humor grew and thrived.

Humor depends on some basic elements to thrive. First, the comic must be in an environment where he or she feels free to be humorous without being condemned, arrested, or ostracized. In the U.S., comics are freer than anywhere in the world. In dictatorships, certain types of humor can be dangerous and cause a person to be arrested, so comics need to be careful. For example, the world recently witnessed where a cartoon about the Prophet Mohammed in a Danish newspaper led radical Muslims to riot, kill, and burn Christian churches in other countries.

Second, comics need to be free to take risks in order to produce good humor. If one is not free to take these risks, and/or fears being harmed because they tackle certain subjects, the humor will be limited, at best. It is my belief that because the U.S. has provided the most open and free environment, including the freedom of speech and expression, we have provided an environment in which humor could grow and develop. It is also true that as a nation we have provided rewards to good humorists, in terms of recognition and money. We like to laugh, we appreciate those who make us laugh, and therefore, we reward them. As a result, we have the greatest body of humor the world has ever seen.

While some who read this will see it as an intellectual stretch to say that our Christian heritage has been a significant factor in the development of our national value of humor, I don't think it is. And, if our humor does come, at least in part, from our Christian heritage and values, it isn't a stretch to believe that this reflects a characteristic of the God in whom Christians believe, and that he indeed laughs, too.

Dark and Inappropriate Humor

This book would not be complete unless the subject of dark, negative, and inappropriate humor was addressed. There is a type of humor that has some very negative aspects and there is a type of humor that is frowned on in scripture. First, let us look at dark humor, which is often referred to as black humor, sick humor, blue humor, or obscene humor.

It is not uncommon in life to find that where there is something positive and good, one can often find a counterfeit product that apes the good, but is evil or bad. Whether it is money, religion, literature, TV, politics, or other enterprises, the bad seems to follow the good and attempts to rob it of its value. So it is with humor.

As an aside, one of the most important books I have read is a book by Will and Ariel Durant entitled *The Lessons of History*. The Durants are perhaps the most prolific writers of world history in the 20th century. After having written 10 volumes on various periods of history, they stepped back and wrote a small, 100-page book on the lessons they believed we should learn from history. It should be noted here that the Durants were openly agnostic in their religious beliefs. One of the remarkable observations of the Durants is that history reveals a continuous battle between good and evil. They say, "If history supports any theology, it would be a dualism . . . a good spirit and an evil spirit battling for control of the universe and men's souls (*The Lessons of History*, Simon and Schuster, 1968, 46)." It seems this dualism reflects itself in humor as well because there is good healthy humor and there is dark, sick, and unhealthy humor.

When humor focuses on people's disabilities, tears people down, pokes fun of individuals, appeals to people's base instincts, demeans a race or ethnic group, or uses filthy, four–letter words to get laughs, it goes over the line and becomes negative and counterproductive. Comedian Buddy Hackett, whose comedy often skirted the line between appropriate and inappropriate humor, once said that every comedian knows when they have crossed the line during a performance because the quality of the audience's laughter changes. The laughter, Hackett says, becomes muted and stifled as people are shocked, have their good senses challenged, and wonder whether they should laugh or not. Some comedians, however, develop reputations for this sick or dark humor and constantly "push the envelope" to see what they can get away with. It's not a coincidence that some comedians who have used this type of humor have also lived broken lives and died prematurely. Examples include Sam Kinnison, Lenny Bruce, and John Belushi.

Lenny Bruce, whose real name was Leonard Schneider, was a Jewish comedian born in 1925. Bruce's comedy reflected a troubled life, which included alcohol and drug addiction. He was arrested several times for violating obscenity laws by using foul language in his performances. His tangles with the law were numerous and very public. At one point, when he was in the hospital for a drug overdose, it was reported his language was so foul the nurses refused to enter his room until they taped his mouth shut. Bruce's troubled life ended at age 42, reportedly from another drug overdose. It seems Lenny's humor reflected a deeply troubled spirit. His humor may well have been his way of trying to escape from the dark side of his inner being.

It is axiomatic that people's speech and/or humor ultimately reflects what is in their heart and reveals a bit of what is at the core of their inner self. Lenny Bruce spewed forth a bitterness and filth that was sad to see. His comedy, which often focused on social issues like nuclear testing, abortion, and illegal drugs, attracted a significant national following. His battles with authorities over freedom of speech issues made him a hero to some, but to most he was a terribly sad and troubled soul.

Sam Kinnison was a child preacher in the Pentecostal Church. He fell away from his faith and became a comedian, known for his filthy language and dark humor. His life became plagued by alcohol and drugs. He spewed forth filth from the core of his being, similar to that of Lenny Bruce. Ironically it seemed that Sam Kinnison had just cleaned up his life and act when he was killed in a head-on automobile accident. It was ironic because the driver of the other car was drunk. Kinnison died near Las Vegas, Nevada at the age of 38.

John Belushi was a very funny guy and a standout on *Saturday Night Live* for several years. But off TV, his private comedy acts left much to be desired. He used blue language and offbeat topics. His life was plagued with alcohol and drug use. His unhappy life was reflected in his dark humor, and he died at 33 of a heroin overdose.

Another of the comedians who practiced dark humor was Theodore Gottleib, known as Brother Theodore. Gottleib struck the fancy of Merv Griffin and appeared 36 times on his variety show. Brother Theodore, who survived the holocaust, had monologues filled with guilt, frustration, and existential fear. His life was troubled and included having his wife run off with his best friend, taking their son with her. Brother Theodore lived in New York City and practiced his comedy at the 13th Street Theatre for many years. While his humor dealt with dark issues, he did not have the same problems Lenny Bruce and others had with filthy language. One of Brother Theodore's famous lines was, "Dear God, if you exist, help me, and if you don't exist, help me anyway."

While most comedians, as mentioned earlier, seem to benefit from the healthy, life-extending properties of humor, this does not seem to apply to those who use dark humor. Many, as noted above, die early of a reckless lifestyle. Brother Theodore seems to be an exception, as he died in 2000 at the age of 93. At one point, he said of himself, "Madness is a very healthy sickness. If it were not for my madness, I would have gone insane." In that statement we get a glimpse of Brother Theodore's black, self-deprecating humor.

There are a number of comedians, some very much alive, who tend to practice sarcasm, social criticism, demeaning others, and focusing on the ills of society, but who do not go to the same extremes that a Lenny Bruce did. We have comedians such as Mort Sahl, George Carlin, Al Franken, and others who are more mainstream, but who tend toward the dark end of the comedic spectrum. These comedians have a following, particularly among those with the same political persuasion, who love to hear their political foes torn down. In short, these comedians have a political agenda and seek to further it by tearing down their opponents with sarcasm and humor.

There are also comedians like Mark Russell, David Letterman, Jay Leno, and others who make humor about current events and political figures, but do so in good fun and without a raw political agenda that conveys a hate for those they joke about. The humor practiced by these comedians is usually healthy and follows in the historic vein of a Will Rogers. After all, in a free and open democracy, good humor is an important element in making public discourse open and attractive. Also, it seems to me that in a democratic and open society, it is good to laugh at, as well as with, our leaders at times to keep them a bit humble and remind them they are the people's servants, not their untouchable bosses.

Don Rickles is a particularly unique comedian in that his whole comedic approach is to seemingly tear down other people and make fun of their foibles, yet he does it in such a way that no one gets mad at him for doing it. Rickles seems to have the gift of conveying the feeling that, while he's poking fun of someone, he really likes them, and is in no way being hurtful. Rickles used to be a regular on the *Dean Martin Roasts* TV program, which routinely gave people Martin admired the honor of being "roasted" in front of a national TV audience. Rickles roasted others as well as anyone because it fit his style of comedy. In addition, Rickles was so well-known that it was an honor for someone to be the butt of his jokes.

Contrast Don Rickles with an Al Franken and you see a major difference. Even though they both roast people, Franken has a political agenda that is liberal and Democratic. When Franken pokes fun of President Bush or Rush Limbaugh, it is clear he is trying to demean and tear them down. His comments often would be classified as nasty. He clearly disagrees with them politically and does not like them personally. Franken has developed a liberal audience, which likes to hear him poke fun of Republicans, conservatives, and particularly the religious right. In short, while Rickles actually likes the people he spoofs, and it shows, Franken actually dislikes the people he puts down, and that shows, too. In my mind, this distinction is the line between wholesome comedy and negative humor. It may be idealistic, but a malicious tearing down of people, even for humorous or political reasons, steps over the line.

The kind of humor that relies on filthy discourse or curse words to get laughter is also humor that is not healthy. Those who practice this type of humor and/or rely on course sexual content for laughs tear down public morals and give people the impression that using this type of language is appropriate. As with Belushi, Kinnison, and Bruce, mentioned above, this approach to humor frequently points to an internal psychological problem, and the filth that spews forth reflects their inner feelings. This reflects the biblical truth set forth in Matthew 12:33-34 where we read . . . "For out of the overflow of the heart the mouth speaks. The good man brings good things out of the good stored up in him, and the evil man brings evil things out of the evil stored in him." Unfortunately, there are many comedians plying their trade in the comedy clubs across America, on cable TV, and on satellite radio, where their filth is permitted, that display these "evil things" to the detriment of us all.

Many comedians use jokes about male/female relationships and sex to get laughs. Some of these jokes are harmless and healthy, however, many go over the line of decency. Poking fun of adultery and sexual indiscretions can have a very negative impact on people. To laugh about adultery and unfaithfulness tends to convey a respectability of that conduct it doesn't deserve. The moral decline in America is due in part to our willingness to laugh at conduct that is inappropriate, and to the Christian, sinful. It is easy to skate over the line between appropriate and inappropriate humor. I must confess I have done so at times, in search of a laugh. It is wrong, however, and it coarsens the sexual behavior that God has intended to be beautiful and healthy in the marriage relationship. This is an area where Christians can easily be tempted and need to be on constant guard.

There is also in America a brand of humor that is aimed at ethnic and racial groups. At one extreme, this humor can be innocent and funny, but it can easily cross the line. Everyone has heard jokes about the Irish, Polish, Dutch, Jews, etc. Much of this humor tends to feed off of stereotypical generalizations. For example, Irish jokes often focus on their drinking, Jewish jokes on their handling of money, etc. In the town where I grew up, there was a Polish side of town and a Dutch side of town (Grand Rapids, Michigan). Sometimes you could hear the same joke on both sides of town, but in one the object of the joke was a Dutchman, while on the other side of town is was a Pole.

In the mid-20th century one of the most popular radio programs was *Amos and Andy*. Later, it became a popular TV series, however, the stereotypical behavior of blacks it was founded on was harmful and inaccurate. When the civil rights movement developed, it became clear that the humor of *Amos and Andy* was harmful to blacks and was presenting a stereotype of black life that was wrong. The TV and radio programs haven't been heard of since. A similar situation led to the demise of the black-faced comedians in the minstrel shows that were popular in earlier times. It is fair to say that if a comedic vehicle or genre presents a false and harmful picture of a racial or ethnic group, it should not be used. Any humor that demeans individuals or groups should be classified as dark and inappropriate humor.

The line between healthy and dark humor is sometimes blurred, and may be thought of as more of a "grey area." Sometimes the line might even be in the eye of the beholder. For example, one obese person who is happy with himself/herself might laugh at a joke about fat people, while another might be crushed and offended by the same story. It is far better to avoid all jokes and comments that are aimed at poking fun of individuals or groups, and certainly to avoid using foul language in attempts to get laughs. These are areas of humor that Christian values dictate we avoid. A good rule for Christians is that if there is any doubt at all about the appropriateness of a joke, don't tell it. Better a missed laugh than a harmful experience.

This black side of humor is a stark contrast to the clean, healthy humor chronicled in earlier chapters. Given the earlier discussion on the effect of humor on healing and longevity, it should be noted here that several of the comedians using, dark, obscene, or filthy humor lived lives that were too short. Pertinent evidence of this fact are the short lives and tragic deaths of comics like Lenny Bruce who died at 40, Sam Kinnison at 38, and John Belushi at 33. They went over the line of decency to get laughs, versus the long, happy, and productive lives of the comedians who used clean humor. It seems the core of the lives of those who died early was in poor order, which led to the abuse of alcohol and illegal drugs, and shortened their lives. Their comedy seemed to reflect their darkness and internal pain, and while they were ostensibly funny men, the laughter could not cover up the blackness and evil inside.

The apostle Paul speaks at one point to some of these issues. In Ephesians 5:4 Paul says, "Nor should there be obscenity, foolish talk, or coarse joking, which are out of place, but rather thanksgiving." Matthew Henry in his commentary (*Matthew Henry's Commentary In One Volume, Genesis to Revelation*, Zondervan Publishing House, 1960.), suggests that this comment by Paul in no way is prohibiting innocent and inoffensive jesting (Henry, 653). But Paul clearly indicates there is a line that delineates "innocent jesting" from "coarse jesting."

It seems clear that when people jest or make light of very serious matters of faith, they go over a line. Their speech and jesting becomes what we have come to call sacrilegious. Such speech or humor suggests a lack of reverence, or even a contempt for things regarded as sacred. For example, if one were to joke about Christ's Crucifixion, the Bible, the sacraments, salvation, or other basic tenets of the faith, it would be inappropriate and what Paul would consider "coarse joking." Joking about something tends to reduce it in importance. When we do it, we say we "make light" of something. Christians need to avoid this type of humor about critical matters of faith.

Related to the previous point is a type of humor that pokes fun of or makes light of behavior that is sinful to the Christian. Consider, for example, jokes about adultery, divorce, abortion, homosexuality, and killing. There is a tendency when joking about topics like this to see them as less sinful than they really are, and to make them almost acceptable. Christians should be mindful of this and avoid humor that either demeans that which is holy, or which makes light of that which is sinful. Modern American TV does the latter to the detriment of the Christian values upon which our country was founded. Adultery, fornication, homosexuality, and all manner of sexual perversion are laughed at, and thereby made less serious than they really are, and, in fact, are made to seem like the norm for sexual behavior in society.

The fact that sometimes the lines between the good and bad types of humor are hard to detect is why some of our Christian forefathers recommended avoiding humor altogether, in order to avoid the problems mentioned above. I would agree with Matthew Henry that Paul was not prohibiting innocent or harmless jesting. He was just suggesting there was a negative type of humor that we as Christians must recognize and avoid.

In summary, there is evil in the world as well as good. The existence of negative, dark, black, or inappropriate humor should not surprise anyone, particularly Christians. The presence of negative and harmful humor, however, does not negate the positive effects of good, clean humor, nor should it in any way impact the fact that clean, wholesome humor can be Christian, positive, and a characteristic of God. When we compare the outcomes of healthy humor with negative humor, I believe we see the contrast between good and evil, and between God and Satan.

Conclusions Regarding God and Humor

So how are we to perceive God and humor? As mentioned earlier, as humans we are limited in our capacity to perceive God because he is unique and beyond our experiential and perceptual capabilities to understand. We have known nothing like him in our human experience, yet God has, nevertheless, revealed aspects of himself to us in a variety of ways. In the Bible, we read a good deal about God. For example, in Job 38-39, God reveals much of himself to Job and to us. We can also infer much about God as we read how he dealt with various individuals and situations — from Genesis and Adam and Eve, through Revelations, to the end of time. And, of course, we can learn much about God from Jesus Christ.

We find that the concept God chose to give us a better understanding of him is that of a perfect father. This concept is introduced briefly in the Old Testament in Isaiah 9:6 and Malachi 2:10, and is greatly magnified in the New Testament. Jesus referred to God the Father over 200 times. In addition, the Bible gives us a good deal of information about God. Here are some of the things we are told about him:

1. He is spirit (John 4:24).
2. He is omnipotent (all powerful) (Matthew 19:26).
3. He is omniscient (all knowing) (Matthew 10:29).
4. He is omnipresent (everywhere present) (Psalm 139: 1-24).
5. He is holy (John 17:11).
6. He is righteous (John 17:25).
7. He is loving (John 3:16-23).
8. He is good (Matthew 6:16, 28-30; 10:29-30).
9. He is just (Isaiah 45:21).

So we get a picture of God as holy, just, and righteous, but also as loving and good, all in perfect balance. Such a father must be full of peace and joy, and as such, he must logically have a sense of humor and capacity to laugh. Throughout this book, we have examined several reasons why God laughs, which are as follows:

1. The Bible says God laughs, and it is clear that Jesus Christ, who was God incarnate, laughed and had a sense of humor.

2. The nature of laughing is positive and good. It has healing properties and is highly beneficial. These positive characteristics associate laughing with "good" and thereby with God.

3. There is a vast amount of humor in God's creation. Only a God with a sense of humor could produce the laughs we get from his handiwork.

4. There is humor among great Christians, and a good deal of humor among God's people and in his church. If humor and laughing were by nature evil, that would not be so.

5. America is a Christian nation, and no nation in the history of the world has developed such a rich body of humor. If humor and Christianity were opposed, that would not be the case. Conversely, I believe our nation's Christian character, with its

emphasis on freedom, has facilitated the development of our heritage of humor.

Some readers might look at all this evidence and still say, "so what?" The "so what" is, I believe, that we learn from all of this that our God has a side of himself we often do not stop to see, and which is exceptionally attractive. Not only does he love, but he laughs too. Not only is he a righteous judge, but he is kind, caring, and approachable, too. The sometimes somber and angry God we see judging evil and disobedient children has a compassionate and humorous side as well. Those from Christian traditions that overemphasize the harsh side of God, or individuals caught up in debilitating guilt, should spend some time factoring the truth of the humorous, compassionate side into their concept of God lest they miss some of the comfort, peace, and joy a full-balanced knowledge of God can bring.

It is hard to love someone you truly fear, and while we need to fear sin and judgment, we do not need to fear God. We should fear missing knowing a loving and compassionate God, and we should fear missing an eternity with him. But we should never fear a relationship with a loving, heavenly father who loves us, who forgives us when we fall short, and who wants nothing more than to spend an eternity with us.

Jesus teaches us that God loves us so much he redeemed us through the sacrifice of his only son. The parable of the lost sheep, the lost coin, and the lost son (Luke 15:1-32) all teach us how much our heavenly father wants every one of us to be a part of eternity with him. A good and loving earthly father will do anything possible to save a son or daughter, and so will our heavenly father. We just need to acknowledge him and follow his loving guidance. The only way we can fail in this life is to reject God and commit the unpardonable sin (Matthew 12:28-29, Mark 3:31-32) of blaspheming and rejecting God's spirit. This action separates us from God and prevents any relationship. All other sins can and will be forgiven, if we but ask. A loving father cannot reject a son or daughter, no matter how bad, if they acknowledge him, accept him, love him, and want a relationship with him. Our heavenly father does nothing less.

We are helped to understand something of God by thinking of a perfect human father. When we do this, we see strength and compassion; we see truth and justice, as well as mercy; we see anger at sin and disobedience tempered with forgiveness and love; and we also see humor and laughter. Who couldn't be attracted to a God like this? What loving father wouldn't do everything possible to see to it that his children turned out to be the best they could be, and have everything good they might want? God wants only the very best for us.

It's also true that in this life there are forces competing for our loyalty. Satan has some freedom to try and lead us astray. Feelings of inferiority, fear, and guilt come from that direction. If, however, we look to our loving Heavenly Father for help and guidance, the evil one can't possibly win in our lives. We're guaranteed a marvelous victory.

The only fear anyone should have regarding God is that they should fall to the temptation of denying he is, in fact, who he says he is. If we avoid this unpardonable sin, accept Jesus Christ, and do our best to follow God's guidelines and live for him, we have nothing to fear and everything to look forward to. Because if we truly know God, we will be filled with peace, joy, and laughter here, and when we get to our heavenly home, we will know a joy and laughter so profound we can't imagine the extent of it here. And when we hear a full, hearty, heavenly laugh from our God, we'll smile, too, and know we're truly home for good.

Now, if you want to enjoy some earthly laughter and gain some of the healthy benefits that go with it, go to Appendix A, where some examples of good, clean humor await you.

Appendix B contains a discussion of a phenomenon that has become an issue, particularly in the charismatic movement. It is the phenomenon of holy laughter. There are conflicting opinions in the church about whether this is a manifestation of the Holy Spirit or of Satan. Since this is a book about God and laughing, it was deemed necessary to include a discussion of holy laughter. You may want to read Appendix B and decide for yourself.

Appendix A
Examples of
Clean Humor

The following stories are intended to be examples of good, clean humor. Many of the stories below are jokes I've heard and used for years. The reader may have heard some of them, or versions of them, but a good story, like a good song, deserves to be repeated. If as you read these jokes you get a good laugh or two, they will have served their purpose by causing some endorphins to circulate through your body and perhaps add a bit to your mental and physical health. Read, enjoy, laugh, and feel better, because I'm convinced God has created laughter for our benefit. Remember, God created us in his image, and if we laugh, he most certainly does, too. And if God does it, it must be good.

1. **The Baptist Lumberman** — A Baptist lumberman was working in a small Oregon town when he was caught stealing lumber. His boss told him he would have to go to the local church and confess his sin to the pastor. The man protested because he said he was Baptist and the only church in town was Catholic. The boss said he had to go or lose his job, so the lumberman went. After confessing, the priest told him he would have to make a novena to have his sins forgiven. The lumberman responded, "I don't know what a novena

is, but if you can get me the blueprints, I know where I can get the lumber."

2. **The Atlanta Airport** — A new air traffic controller had just come on the job when a pilot called in and said, "Atlanta, this is United Flight 250 from Chicago. I'm in the area and would like permission to land." The controller responded, "Welcome y'all to Atlanta. You are clear to land on runway number 1 from the north." The United pilot acknowledged the message and left the channel open. A minute later, he heard another pilot call in and say, "Atlanta, this is Delta flight 100 from New Orleans I'm in the area and would like permission to land." The controller responded saying, "Welcome y'all to Atlanta. You are clear to land on runway Number 1 from the south." The United pilot quickly called back to the tower and said, "Atlanta, Atlanta, you've just cleared another pilot to land on the same runway you've cleared us to land on and he's coming from the opposite direction. What should I do?" There was a long pause and then the controller came on the channel and said, "Y'all be careful now, ya hear!"

3. **The Alzheimer's Patients** — A doctor had three Alzheimer's patients down at the retirement home. He would go there every couple of weeks and see how they were doing. One Monday he was there and got the three men in a room and said he was going to give each of them a math test to see how they were doing. They said that was fine. He went to the first and said, "John, how much is 3x3?" John thought for a moment and finally said, "The answer is 152." The doctor didn't say anything, but he went to the second man and said, "George, how much is 3x3?" George thought for a moment and said, "Tuesday." Well, the doctor was getting discouraged, but he went to the third man and asked, "Sam, how much is 3x3?" Sam shot right back, "The answer is nine, doctor." The doctor said, "That's right, Sam, that's wonderful. You got it right. By the way, Sam, how did you get your answer?" Sam responded, "It was easy, I just subtracted Tuesday from 152."

4. **The Devil in Costume** — A man and his wife were on their way to a Halloween party in the country and they got lost. He was dressed as Satan and she as an angel. They came to a small country church that was having a revival service. The wife told her husband to go up to the church and ask for directions, which he did. The door was stuck so he kicked it hard. The door flew open with a loud noise and there stood the man in his costume, dressed as the devil. This scared the congregation, and they flew out of the church in every direction, except for one woman. She was elderly and quite a bit overweight. She tried to get out through a window and couldn't make it. The man walked over to her to get directions, but before he could speak she said, "Sir, I've been a member of this church for 40 years. I've been a member of the choir, I've taught Sunday school, and I've been a member of the Woman's Guild, but I want you to know, I've been on your side the whole time."

5. **The Bathroom** — A Sunday school teacher asked her preschool class if they knew where God lived. One little boy raised his hand and said he knew. So the teacher asked him where God lived. He responded, "God lives in my bathroom at home." The teacher said, "How do you know?" The little boy replied, "Because every morning my dad stands outside the bathroom door and shouts, 'my God, are you still in there?' "

6. **The Substitute** — A young seminary student was called early one Sunday morning to go and substitute for a nearby pastor who had become ill overnight. The student hurried off to the church and found himself in the pulpit. That morning, he told the congregation he was a substitute. When he said it, he realized he had been taught to illustrate major points he was making. He then told the congregation a substitute would be similar to putting a piece of wood in a window if the glass had been broken out. The wood would be a substitute for the glass, as he was a substitute for their pastor. He went on and gave his sermon, and was greeting people at the back of the church, as they were leaving, when a little old lady came up to him and said,

"Young man, I listened to your sermon carefully, and as far as I am concerned, you were no substitute. As far as I'm concerned, you were a real pane."

7. **The Pitcher** — A little boy was learning to play baseball. One day, his father came home to find his son in the front yard by himself throwing the ball up in the air and trying to hit it when it came down. The little boy was missing the ball every time. Finally, the father went up to him and said, "You're not hitting the ball too well, are you?" The little boy responded by saying, "No, I'm not a very good hitter, but I'm a great pitcher, aren't I?"

8. **The Race** — Two fellows were out walking in the mountains when they came around a corner and found themselves face-to-face with a huge grizzly bear. The one fellow immediately sat down and began changing his shoes, putting on his lighter running shoes. The other fellow said, "What are you doing? We can't outrun this bear!" The first fellow replied, "I know we can't out run the bear, but all I have to do is outrun you."

9. **The King of the Jungle** — A lion was going through the jungle asking the animals who was king of the jungle. He asked a monkey and a hippo and they both answered correctly that he was. Next, he came to an elephant and asked him. The elephant picked up the lion with his trunk, whirled him about, threw him on the ground, and put his foot on the lion's neck, where upon the lion said, "The next time you don't know the answer, don't get mad!"

10. **The Burglar** — A burglar broke into a home late one night and was moving about in the dark when he heard a voice say, "You'd better leave or Jesus will get you." The burglar turned on his flashlight and shined it at the voice, and saw it was a parrot. He said to the parrot, "Who are you?" The parrot said, "My name is Moses." The burglar said, "Who's crazy enough to name a parrot Moses?" The parrot replied, "The same people who named their 150-pound

rottweiller Jesus."

11. **The Brain Transplant** — A fellow was told he needed a brain transplant and that he could go down to the hospital gift shop and pick out a new brain. The clerk showed him one from a teacher and said it would cost $10,000. She showed him another from a banker, and said it was $15,000. Then she showed him one from a politician and said it would cost $1 million. The man asked how come the politician's brain was so expensive. The clerk replied, "Because the politician's brain has never been used."

12. **The Election** — An election was being held for mayor in a small Irish town of 100 people, 98 of which were Catholics, and two Jewish. Two candidates were running for mayor, one was Catholic and the other was Jewish. When the votes were tallied, the Catholic candidate was elected. The Catholic candidate asked what the vote was and he was told it was 98 to two, whereupon he said, "Boy, you Jews sure are clannish."

13. **The Parking Lot** — A fellow walked into a loan office in downtown New York and asked to borrow $1,000. He said he would leave his $100,000 Rolls Royce as collateral. He got the loan, gave the loan officer his keys, and left. A week later he returned. He repaid the $1,000 and $3.00 in interest on the loan. The loan officer asked him why he would leave his Rolls Royce as collateral for a $1,000 loan. The man replied, "Where else could I park my car for a week in downtown New York for $3.00?"

14. **The History Lesson** — A little black boy hadn't been doing too well in school. One day, his teacher told the class that the next day they were going to have a test on the sayings of famous Americans, and said that if he did well, he'd get a good grade for the quarter. The little black boy went home and studied all night. He came the next morning certain he'd do well and put his academic problems behind him. Just before lunch, the teacher said, "Okay children, I'm going

to give you an oral test now on the sayings of famous Americans. Who can tell me who said, 'The only thing we have to fear is fear itself.' " "The little black boy fired his hand up but the teacher called on a little Mexican girl and said, "Maria, who said that?" Maria answered, "Franklin Roosevelt, teacher." "That's correct, very good. Let's try another. Who said, 'I regret that I have but one life to give to my country?' "Again the little black boy quickly put his hand up but again the teacher called on another little Mexican girl, and said, "Lolita, who said that?" She replied, "Nathan Hale, teacher." "That's wonderful, that's correct," responded the teacher. "Let's try one more before lunch. Who can tell me who said, 'Ask not what your country can do for you, but what you can do for your country?' " Again the little black boy quickly raised his hand up, but again the teacher called upon another. This time, she asked a little Mexican boy saying, "Pablo, who said that?" Pablo quickly said, "John F. Kennedy, teacher." "That's correct, that's wonderful. I can tell you studied. Okay, children it's time to go to lunch." Well, at this point the little black boy was fit to be tied because he'd studied so hard and wasn't called on. He finally lost it and blurted out, "Damn those Mexicans." The teacher quickly turned around and said, "Who said that?" The little black boy responded, "Davy Crockett at the Alamo in 1836."

15. **The Cajun Dog** — A Northerner heard about a remarkable dog down in Louisiana, in Cajun country, and decided to go and see the dog for himself. After inquiring a bit, he found his way to a Cajun who owned the dog. He asked if he could go hunting with the Cajun to see the dog in action. The Northerner asked what the dog's name was and he was told it was pronounced "Fido" but spelled Phideaux. The two men were sitting in a duck blind when the Cajun shot a duck and told Phideaux to get it. The Northerner was amazed to see the dog run across the water, pick up the duck, and bring it back. He was even more amazed when it happened again; the dog again ran across the water and brought another duck back. The Northerner said he'd never seen a dog walk on water before and asked the Cajun

why he didn't advertise the dog's amazing ability and make a lot of money showing him off. The Cajun replied he didn't do it because he was too embarrassed that his dog had never learned to swim.

16. **The Birth of a Calf** — A fellow from New York had grown up and spent his whole life in the city. One day, he decided to drive out into the country to some farms and see how country folk lived. As he was driving along, he saw a farmer hunched over the back of a cow and he looked like he was having trouble. The city fellow stopped, climbed the fence, and asked the farmer if he could help. The farmer said to take hold of a leg and pull. A calf was being born in a breech position and was coming out hind legs first. After a struggle, the little calf was born and staggered to its feet. The city fellow looked on in amazement and then told the farmer that he'd never seen anything like it. Then he said, "By the way, how fast was the little guy going when he hit the big guy?"

17. **The Senior Driver** — A senior citizen took his wife for a drive through the city. Suddenly, he saw a police car behind him, motioning him to pull over. He stopped and the officer came to his window. The policeman said, "Mister, your wife fell out of your car a half mile back." The senior replied, "Oh, thank goodness, I thought I'd gone deaf."

18. **The Violent Hymn** — Little Billy seemed upset at the family's Sunday noon dinner. His mother asked, "What's the trouble, Billy?" Billy said he didn't like the violent hymn they sang in church that morning. "What hymn was that?" his father asked. Billy replied, "The one that goes 'there is a bomb in Gilead.' "

19. **The Hearing Aid** — An elderly gentleman was very hard of hearing. One day, he saw an advertisement for a new hearing aid that claimed to restore 100% of one's hearing. His doctor guided him through the process of getting the new hearing aid and making sure it worked perfectly. A month later, the gentleman had a follow

up with his doctor. The doctor asked how the device was working, and the man said it was working perfectly. Then the doctor said, "Your family must be thrilled that you can hear." The man replied, "Oh, I haven't told them I can hear. I just sit and listen. As a result, I've changed my will three times."

20. **The Robber** — A man was sentenced to ten years in jail for robbing a bank. When he was sentenced, he told the judge he was innocent because when the bank was robbed he was all the way across town robbing a convenience store. "That will now be 20 years," responded the judge.

21. **Dumb Fishermen** — Two men were out fishing and were catching fish right and left. Before they quit for the day, the one said to the other, "Mark this spot and we'll come back tomorrow." When they returned the next day, the one asked the other, "Did you mark the spot?" The other said, "Yes, I did. I put a big 'X' on the bottom of the boat." His friend thought for a moment and then said, "That was stupid, we might not get the same boat."

22. **The Stingy Man** — A woman married to a very stingy man told him one day she was going out window shopping. He said that was okay, but she needed to make sure she didn't buy anything. When she came home with a new dress, he was fit to be tied. "Why did you buy that dress?" he asked. "Well," she answered, "I saw this nice dress and I went in to try it on, and when I did, the devil said, 'It sure looks good on you.'" The husband said, "Right then you should have said, 'Satan get behind me!'" The wife replied, "I did tell him to get behind me, and he said the dress looked good on me from the back, too."

23. **The Rescue** — A man was out walking through the mountains with a friend when he fell into a crevice. His friend said that he'd go for help. Some time later, a rescuer looked over the edge and said, "Everything's okay, I'm from the Red Cross." The man looked up

and said, "Go away, I gave at the office."

24. **Another Rescue** — A man was looking over the edge of a cliff when he slipped and fell. As he was falling, he grabbed on to the branch of a small tree. He immediately yelled out, "Help me! Is there anyone up there?" A voice came back saying, "Yes, I'm God and I'm here." "Well, save me, please," the man said. "Do you have faith," God responded. "Yes, you wouldn't believe how much faith I have. Now please, save me." God said, "If you have faith, let go of the branch and I'll save you." The man hesitated and then yelled, "Is there anyone else up there?"

25. **The Payback** — A lady was at a funeral parlor and observed a friend of hers pause at the casket of the deceased gentleman and put something in the coffin. Her curiosity got the better of her. She took her friend aside and said to her, "Did I see you put something in the coffin?" "Yes, I did," her friend explained. "What was it? The lady asked. "Well," said her friend, "you see, I borrowed $20,000 from the deceased about six months ago and I swore on my honor that I would repay him." "You mean you put $20,000 in that coffin?" the lady said. "Well, not exactly," her friend replied. "I wrote him a check."

26. **The Dying Man** — A doctor had just informed a gentleman he had a fatal illness and there was nothing they could do to help him. The man asked, "How much time do I have?" The doctor replied that he never told people that as a matter of policy. "But you've got to tell me doctor. Please, I have to know." "No," the doctor said, "I can't tell you." But the man persisted and wore the doctor down. Finally, the doctor said, "Let me put it this way, if I were you, I wouldn't buy a bunch of green bananas."

27. **The Snack** — An elderly couple was watching TV one night when the husband offered to get his wife a snack. She said she wanted some popcorn, but insisted he write it down because she said he'd

forget. He refused to write it down and said he was chagrined that she thought he'd forget. Off he went to the kitchen and returned about 15 minutes later with some scrambled eggs for his wife. "See," she said, "I knew you couldn't remember what I wanted. You forgot my toast."

28. **George Burns** — One day, when George Burns was in his late 90s, he was being interviewed by a news reporter. The man said, "Mr. Burns, is it true you smoke several cigars everyday?" "Yes," Burns replied, "I just love cigars." "And, Mr. Burns, is it true that you have one or two martinis every day?" "Oh yes, I love martinis and usually have two every day." "And, Mr. Burns, is it true you frequently chase after younger women?" "Yes, that's true, too. I love younger women, but the older I get, the more difficulty I have remembering what I'm supposed to do when I catch them." The reporter then said, "Mr. Burns, you chase younger women, you smoke cigars, and you drink martinis every day. What does your doctor say about that?" "I don't know," Burns replied, "he's dead."

29. **The Poison** — A man was on his deathbed and felt he had to confess to his wife that he had been unfaithful. He said, "Sweetheart, I must confess to you that I was unfaithful to you recently." She responded, "Yes, I know, that's why I poisoned you."

30. **Getting A Wife** — A little boy in Sunday school had been particularly interested in how humans came into being. The teacher explained that God had created Adam out of the dust, but that God had taken one of Adam's ribs and made Eve for his wife. A week or so later the boy was ill, and his mother asked what was wrong. The little boy said, "I have a pain in my side, I think I'm going to have a wife."

31. **The Runaway** — A neighbor of a little boy noticed that he had his backpack on and kept walking around and around the block. Finally, the neighbor stopped him and inquired, "Johnny, why are

you walking around and around the block?" Johnny replied, "I'm running away from home, but my mother said I couldn't cross the street."

32. **The Senior Olympics** — An 85-year-old man went to his first senior Olympics. On his first day there, he backed into a javelin and won the broad jump.

33. **The Senior Marriage** — A 90-year-old man went to a minister and asked if he would marry him. The minister said that he would first have to ask some questions. The senior said that was fine. The minister asked, "Do you love her?" The man said, "No, I don't." "Well, is she a Christian?" "I don't know," the man responded. "Does she have lots of money?" "I don't know," the man replied again. "Well," the minister said, "If you don't love her, and you don't know if she's a Christian or has money, why on earth would you want to marry her?" The 90-year-old responded, "Because she can drive at night."

34. **The Gorilla** — A man applied for a job at the zoo. He was told they didn't have an opening, but the man was desperate and persisted. Finally, the zoo manager said that their gorilla had just died and it was a big attraction, so if the man would dress up like a gorilla and perform for the people until they could get a new gorilla he would let him do that. The man was thrilled to have work and did a wonderful job of entertaining those visiting the zoo. One day, he was swinging from branch to branch in a tree next to the lion's den, and he slipped and fell into the lion's enclosure. The man tried to back away slowly as the lion approached; he didn't want to yell out and give himself away. He couldn't get out, however, and finally, as the lion got very close he yelled, "Help!" The lion looked at him and said, "Shut up, you fool, or you'll get us both fired."

35. **The Devil Appears** — During the sermon at a church service one Sunday morning, there was a sharp lightening flash and a loud clap of thunder. Suddenly, the pastor was gone, and in his place

stood Satan himself. The people were frightened and flew out of the church in every direction—all that is, except one elderly gentleman, who sat in the second row with his legs crossed, acting as if nothing happened. Satan looked down and said to him, "Don't you know who I am?" "Oh yes, I know who you are," the man replied. "Well, aren't you afraid of me?" "No, I'm not afraid of you," the man said. "Well, why aren't you afraid of me?" asked Satan. The man replied, "Because I've been married to your sister for 40 years."

36. The Outhouse — An elderly lady whose husband had died lived on a farm. She told her only grandson that he could have the farm if he would fix it up and allow her to live there the rest of her life. The grandson was thrilled and he threw himself into fixing the place up. He remodeled the house and added a small apartment on the back for his grandmother. He tore down the old barn and chicken coop and built new ones. One day, he was standing in the barnyard and he realized that the only thing he hadn't replaced was the old outhouse with the half moon on the door. He decided it would be better to just blow it up and get rid of it. He got some dynamite, set the charge, took the fuse back by the barn, and lit the fuse. As the fuse neared the outhouse, much to his horror, he saw his grandmother running across the barnyard straight for the outhouse. He yelled at her, but she was hard of hearing. Just as his grandmother sat down, the outhouse blew up. His grandmother was blown up in the air and landed on her back, right in front of her grandson. She got up, straightened herself up, looked at her grandson, and said, "Wow, that was something—it must have been something I ate."

37. The Hero — An elderly gentleman was on a Caribbean cruise. One day, he was standing by the railing when a beautiful, young lady fell overboard. A minute later, the elderly gentleman splashed down near her, swam over, and held her up until the launch came and took them back aboard the ship. Well, the elderly gentleman was the hero of the ship and the captain decide to give a party that night to honor his bravery. When the party was in full swing, someone suggested they should hear from the hero. The man said no, he didn't give speeches, and he would rather not. By then the people were clapping and calling for him, and he realized he would have to say something. He approached the microphone and the crowd went totally silent, waiting for the words of wisdom from their hero. The man stepped to the microphone and said, "Okay, who pushed me?"

38. **The Twins** — A psychologist had twin boys. One twin was an incurable optimist and the other was a pessimist. When Christmas came, the psychologist decided to put the twins to the acid test. For the pessimist, he filled up a room with toys, and for the optimist he filled up a room with horse manure. When Christmas morning dawned, he sent each to their assigned room to get their Christmas presents. Soon the pessimist returned downcast, saying he looked at all the toys and there was nothing there he wanted. When the optimist didn't come back, the father went down to the room of manure. Outside he heard his son happily shoveling manure and saying to himself, "With all this manure, I just know there's a pony around here somewhere."

39. **The Frog** — An elderly gentleman was walking in the woods one day when he saw a frog on the path. He picked the frog up and was looking at it when the frog said to him, "If you'll give me a kiss, I'll turn into a beautiful princess." The gentleman thought for a moment and replied saying, "Thanks anyway, but I'd rather have a frog."

40. **The Crying Senior** — An 80-year-old man was sitting on a park bench crying his eyes out. A lady came along and tried to comfort him. She said, "Why are you crying?" The man replied, "Because I have a beautiful house with a swimming pool and a three-stall garage." The lady thought he'd misunderstood and said again, "Why are you crying?" This time the gentleman said, "Because I have a beautiful wife half my age, who is kind and loving and has a

remarkable figure." The lady thought she'd try one more time, so she said, "Sir, why are you crying?" He replied, "Because I just bought three beautiful cars—a Mercedes, a Jaguar, and a Porsche." Now the lady was frustrated and finally said, "Sir, why are you crying when you seem to have everything? You have a beautiful home, a gorgeous wife, and three wonderful, new cars?" The man responded, "I'm crying because I can't remember where I live."

41. The Bird Test — A young man was taking an ornithology class (study of birds) in college. The teacher in the large class said that on Friday, they would have a very important test. The young man decided to study and ace the test. He assumed the teacher would give them pictures of birds and ask the students to identify them. When he got the test, instead of pictures of birds, all the class got were pictures of bird's feet. The young man protested to the teacher. He told her she should change the test. She refused. He said, "I won't take the test, it's unfair." She said, "If you don't take the test, you'll fail." He said, "I don't care, I won't take it." She said, "Okay, you'll fail, by the way, what is your name?" At that, the young man took off his shoes and socks, looked right at the teacher, held up his foot, and said, "Here, you tell me who I am."

42. The Preacher — A young man on a farm in Iowa was trying to decide what he should do with his life. One day, he was in the field and prayed God would show him what he should be. Just then, he looked up and saw the letters PC in the cloud formation. He thought, God wants me to Preach Christ. So he went to college and seminary, and became a pastor. He was literally the worst pastor they had ever seen. He was confused because he really thought that was his calling. He went to the head of the seminary and told him of his problems and also explained how he had received his calling. The seminary president replied, "I think you made a mistake. That PC you saw didn't mean Preach Christ, it meant Plow Corn."

43. Talk with Moses — President George W. Bush was waiting to give a speech when he spotted a man he thought was Moses. He sent a Secret Service agent over to the man to see if it really was Moses, and to tell him he wanted to speak to him. A few minutes later, the agent came back. President Bush said, "Was he Moses, as I thought?" The agent said, "Yes, he's Moses all right, but he won't talk to you. He said that the last time he spoke to a bush he had to spend 40 years in the wilderness."

44. The Church Attendee — An elderly gentleman suddenly stopped attending church. The pastor became concerned and went to visit him. He said, "John, you've seldom missed church in your whole life, but you haven't been there for a month. "Are you ill?" No, I'm feeling fine," the man replied. "Well, is there a problem with my sermons?" asked the pastor. "No, I really like them." "Well, John, why haven't you been to church?" John then offered, "When I was 90, I thought God would take me home. When I hit 95, I was sure he'd take me. Now that I'm 100, I don't want to go to church and remind him I'm still around."

45. Guessing The Age — An elderly gentleman approached an elderly lady in his retirement home and asked her if she could guess how old he was. She said she could if he took off his shirt. After taking his shirt off, he asked her again how old he was. She said she'd tell him, if he took off his pants. Soon the poor fellow was standing before her totally naked. "Well, how old am I?" he asked. "You're 97," the lady replied. "That's right, that's amazing," he said. "How did you know?" "Because you told me yesterday," she replied.

46. The Atheist Teacher — An atheist teacher was determined to prove to her class that there was no God and that evolution was the correct theory. She asked a boy named Billy the following questions: "Billy, do you see the grass outside?" "Yes, teacher," he replied. "Do you see the trees?" "Yes, teacher, I can." "And tell me, Billy, as you look at the sky, do you see God?" "No, teacher, I can't see God." The teacher then said, "So, that proves there is no God, and the theory of evolution is a correct theory." A little girl in the back of the room put up her hand and said, "Teacher, may I ask Billy some questions?" The teacher said she could. The little girl began, "Billy, do you see the grass outside?" "Yes," Billy replied. "And, Billy, do you see the clouds?" Billy, by this time, was a bit frustrated from answering the same questions, but he said, "Yes, I can see the clouds." "And, Billy," said the little girl, "can you see our teacher?" "Yes," Billy said, "I can see our teacher." The little girl then said, "Billy, can you see our teacher's brain?" "No" Billy said, "I can't see her brain." The little girl then said, "Based on what we've been taught today, she doesn't have one."

47. **The Pastor's Visit** — A new pastor was visiting the homes of his parishioners. At one house, he got no answer when he knocked, so he wrote on a card Revelations 3:20, which reads: "Behold I stand at the door and knock," and he put the card in the door. When the offering was taken up the next Sunday, the pastor found a card in the collection plate from the parishioner, which simply said, "Genesis 3:10." When the pastor looked it up it read: "I heard your voice in the garden, and I was afraid for I was naked."

48. **The Lord's Army** — A pastor was greeting those leaving an Easter church service. He said to one man, who seldom attended, "You need to join the Lord's army!" The man replied, "I'm already in the Lord's army, pastor." "Well," said the pastor, "how come I only see you at Christmas and Easter?" The man replied, "That's because I'm in the secret service."

49. **The Poker Game** — Six retired Floridians were playing poker in their condo clubhouse when Meyerwitz lost $500 on a single hand. He clutched his chest and dropped dead. To show respect for their fallen comrade, the five who were left continued playing standing up. Finkelstein finally looked around and said, "So, who's going to tell his wife?" The five decided to draw straws, and Goldberg got the short one. The others advised him to be discreet and gentle,

and to not make the situation any worse than it was. Goldberg said, "Discreet? I'm the most discreet man you will ever meet. Discretion is my middle name. Leave it to me." So, Goldberg went over to the Myerwitz home and knocked on the door. The wife answerd the door and asked what Goldberg wanted. Goldberg said, "Your husband just lost $500 in our poker game and he is afraid to come home." The wife became furious and said, "You tell him to drop dead!" Whereupon Goldberg responded, "Okay, I'll go and tell him right away."

50. **The Educator** — According to a news report, a certain private school in Washington, D.C. was having a problem. A number of 12-year-old girls were putting their lipstick on in the bathroom, after which they would press their lips against the mirror, leaving dozens of lip prints every day. Each night, the maintenance man would clean the mirror only to have the prints return the next day. Finally, the principal decided something had to be done so he called the girls together with the maintenance man in the bathroom. The principal asked the maintenance man to show the girls how he cleaned the glass. The maintenance man dipped his squeegee in the nearest toilet and cleaned the mirror. Since then, there have been no more lip prints on the mirror. There are teachers, and there are educators!

51. **The Bridal Registry** — Jacob, aged 92, and Ann, aged 89, decided to get married. While on a walk one day, they passed a drugstore and Jacob suggested they stop in. Jacob went up to the pharmacist and asked, "Are you the owner?" The pharmacist replied that he was. Jacob then told him they were about to be married and asked, "Do you sell heart medicine?" "Yes, we do," responded the owner. "And do you sell medicine to help one's circulation?" "Yes, we do," the owner again replied. Jacob continued, "How about Viagra, and medicine for arthritis and scoliosis?" "We have all that, too," said the owner. "How about wheelchairs, walkers, vitamins, and sleeping pills?" "We offer everything you've mentioned," replied the owner.

"Great! said Jacob, "We'd like to use this store as our bridal registry."

52. The Tranquil Marriage — A couple was celebrating their 50th wedding anniversary and had a reputation for never having a fight. Someone asked them the secret to their tranquil marriage. The husband responded by saying it all started on their honeymoon. They were taking pack mules down to the bottom of Grand Canyon, when a short way down, the wife's pack mule stumbled and the wife said to the mule, "That's one." A short time later, the mule stumbled again and she said, "That's two." When the mule stumbled a third time, the wife took out a pistol and shot the mule dead. The husband said, "I was furious, and I berated her for being so cruel to an animal. My wife then looked at me and said, 'That's one,' and we haven't had an argument since.'"

53. The Church Jumper — A Dutchman was marooned on a tropical island for ten years when a cruise ship happened by. Some of the crew went ashore, and asked if he wanted to be rescued. He said he did. On the way out to the ship, the captain asked the Dutchman if he had been alone all the time on the island, and the man said he had. The captain then said, "If you were alone, how come there are three huts on the island? The Dutchman replied, "The one in the middle is where I lived, the one on the right is where I go to church, and the one on the left is where I used to go to church."

54. The Free Haircut — A Catholic priest went to get a haircut. When he tried to pay the barber, he was told the haircut was free and that he never charged men of the cloth for haircuts. The next morning, the barber found 12 bottles of beer outside his door. The next day a Baptist minister had his haircut and again the barber refused payment. The next day, he found 12 bottles of root beer outside his door. The next day, a Dutch Reformed minister got his haircut and again the barber explained that he didn't charge men of the cloth. The next morning there were 12 Dutch Reformed ministers outside his door.

55. **The Wedding Cake** — A couple ordered their wedding cake and asked the baker to inscribe on the cake the words from I John 4:8, which reads: "There is no fear in love. But perfect love casts our fear." The baker mistook John 4:8 for I John 4:8 and the cake arrived with the following words: "You have had five husbands and the man you now have is not your husband."

56. **The Doctor's Advice** — An 80-year-old gentleman was jogging alone with a 30-year-old blonde beauty when his cardiologist saw him. The doctor stopped his car and said to the senior, "What are you doing jogging with that blonde?" The man replied he was just following the doctor's orders when he told him to "Get a hot momma and be cheerful." The doctor said, "You didn't hear me correctly. I said you have a heart murmur, be careful."

57. **The Coffee Maker** — A husband and wife were arguing about who should get up and put the coffee pot on in the morning. The husband said cooking was the wife's job, and she should get up and put the pot on. The wife said no, it was his job because the Bible says it's the man's job. The husband said he'd never seen that in the Bible, whereupon his wife opened the Bible to the New Testament and pointed to several pages that read, "Hebrews."

58. **The Definition of a Lie** — A Sunday school class had been memorizing scripture and the teacher wanted to see if the children could apply it, so she asked the children if anyone could define a lie from scripture. A little boy shot up his hand and was called on. He replied, "A lie is an abomination to the Lord, but a very present help in time of trouble."

59. **The Deaf Accountant** — A Mafia Don had an accountant who he was sure had stolen $10 million from him. Since the accountant was deaf, he took a local preacher, who knew sign language, with him to confront the accountant. The Mafia Don said to the preacher, "Ask him where the $10 million dollars are he stole from me." The

accountant signed back to the preacher, "I don't know what he's talking about." The Don then pulled out a pistol and put it to the temple of the accountant, and told the pastor to ask him again. The pastor signed to the accountant, "He'll kill you for sure if you don't tell him where the money is." The accountant signed back to the pastor saying, "Okay, okay, the money is buried behind my garage in a brown briefcase." The Mafia Don asked the pastor, "What did he say?" What did he say?" The preacher answered, "He says you don't have the guts to pull the trigger."

60. The Lengthy Sermon — A minister got carried away on Sunday morning and preached well past his usual time. When he realized it he said, "I'm sorry I preached so long. I'll be finished in just a bit. You see, I left my watch at home." From the back of the church came a voice which said, "There's a calendar behind you."

61. The Trip to Israel — A man decided to take a trip to Israel with his wife. When the wife insisted that her mother go with them, the man reluctantly consented. While in Israel, his mother-in-law died. An Israeli undertaker asked the man whether he wanted his mother-in-law buried in Israel for $500 or shipped back to the U.S. for burial, which would cost $5,000. The man said he wanted her shipped back to the U.S. The undertaker then asked, "Why would you pay $5,000 to ship her back when we could give her a very nice burial here for $500?" The man replied, "You buried a man here 2,000 years ago and he rose from the dead in three days—I can't take that chance."

62. The Final Ride — A man said that he wanted to die peacefully and quick, just like his grandfather—not screaming and yelling like the others in his grandfather's car.

63. The New Song — A little boy came home from Sunday school and told his mother they had learned a new song about Andy. "A song about Andy? "his mother asked. "Yes," he replied, "Andy walks with me, Andy talks with me, Andy tells me I am his own."

64. **The Auto Repair** — A pastor took his car in to be repaired and said to the mechanic, "Please take it easy with the bill, you know I am a poor preacher." The mechanic replied, "I know, I heard you preach last Sunday."

65. **The Prayer** — A pastor was invited over for a Sunday dinner to a member's home. He was asked to say the blessing over the dinner, which he gladly did. When he had finished, little Johnny said approvingly, "You don't pray so long when you're hungry, do you?"

66. **The Temple** — A Sunday school teacher asked the class where Solomon's Temple was located. A little boy put his hand up and said, "I know teacher, on the side of his head."

67. **The Red Lights** — Two little, old ladies were in a big car. They could hardly see over the dashboard. The one in the passenger seat thought they had just run a red light. A short time later, they went through another red light and the passenger said to her friend, "Emma, we just ran two red lights." Emma replied, "Oh shoot, you mean I'm driving?"

68. **Getting to Heaven** — A Sunday school teacher had been teaching her five year olds about salvation and decided to give them a test. She said, "Class, can you get to heaven by helping other people?" The class said, "No, teacher." "Good. Can you get to heaven by being good?" "No, teacher," the class again responded. "That's wonderful, you're right again. Now, who can tell me how you get to heaven?" Little Johnny piped up and said, "Well, first you have to be dead."

69. **Dressing For Church** — A visitor went into a church service dressed in jeans and a sloppy shirt. He seemed dirty, and when he sat down, people moved away from him. After the service, the

minister took him aside and said, "Sir, we'd like you to come back, but before you do, please talk to God about how to dress when you come to our church." The man left, and a week later he showed up in the same clothes. People again shunned him. After the service, the pastor took him aside again and said, "I asked you to talk to God about how to dress in church here. Didn't you do that?" The man said, "Yes, I talked to God as you asked." "Well, what did God say," asked the pastor. "God said he didn't know what people should wear here because he's never been in your church."

70. **Finding Heaven** — Billy Graham tells this story about himself. Early in his ministry he was preaching in a small town during the week, and the afternoon before the service, he wrote a letter. Deciding he wanted to mail it, he left the hotel to find the post office. When he couldn't find it, he approached a small boy and asked if he could tell him where the post office was. The little boy told him. Billy Graham thanked him and then said, "Son, I'm preaching tonight at the Baptist church. Come to the service and I'll tell you how to get to heaven." The little boy responded, "I don't think I'll come. You don't even know where the post office is."

71. **The Chewing Gum Fix** — An elderly grandma was taking her first airplane flight. It was a cross-country flight. When they reached their cruising altitude, she complained to the stewardess that her ears were popping. The flight attendant smiled, gave her some chewing gum, and said the gum should take care of the problem. When they landed, the elderly lady said to the stewardess, "The chewing gum worked fine, but how do I get the gum out of my ears?"

72. **The Tailgater** — A woman was tailgating another car when the car ahead stopped suddenly as a traffic light turned yellow. The woman was furious that the car had stopped because she wanted to get through the light before it turned red. She yelled at the driver, gave him the finger, and screamed obscenities at him. A moment later, a policeman came to her window and arrested her. He took

her to the police station and checked her out. After a time, the policeman came up to her, apologized for detaining her, and said she was free to go. She asked, "Why did you bring me in?" The policeman said, "I noted that your car had stickers on it that said 'Jesus Saves' and 'Follow me to Sunday School,' and that you had a license place with a fish on it. When I observed your behavior at the stoplight, I assumed you had stolen the car."

73. **The Magician** — A little boy was being registered for his first Sunday school class. The teacher took his name and then asked the little boy what his father's occupation was. The little boy said, "He's a magician." The teacher responded, "Oh, that's interesting. What's his best trick?" The boy said, "It's the one where he saws people in half." The teacher then continued to complete the registration form saying, "Do you have any brothers or sisters?" The little boy answered, "Yes, I have one half-brother and one half-sister."

74. **The Prayer Request** — A lady went up to her pastor one Sunday morning and requested a prayer for her pancreas. The minister said that he did not pray for specific organs of the body. The lady said, "Yes, you do. Last Sunday I heard you pray for a loose liver."

75. **The Terrorist** — An American tourist was told not to go to Belfast, Ireland because of the problems between the Catholics and Protestants there and the terrorist activities. He decided to go anyway, and while walking past an alleyway one evening, a man grabbed him and pulled him into the dark and said, "Are you Catholic or Protestant?" The poor tourist didn't know who was holding him or what he should say, but he finally had a bright idea and answered, "I'm neither—I'm Jewish." Whereupon his attacker said, "Ah, faith and begorrah, I must be the luckiest Arab in Belfast."

76. **The Mother Superior** — A 98-year-old mother superior of an order of nuns was dying. The nuns of her order were gathered about her bedside. One offered her a glass of warm milk, but the

dying mother superior wouldn't drink it. One of the nuns took the glass of milk into the kitchen and started to pour it out when she remembered someone had given the order a fine bottle of Irish whiskey. She poured the whiskey into the glass with the remaining milk and took it back to her dying leader. She put the glass to the dying nun's mouth and she sipped a bit. She then sipped more, and in short order had drained the glass. A few moments later, a nun leaned over the bed and said, "Mother, is there some advice you can give us before you leave us?" The mother superior opened her eyes and said, "Yes, don't ever sell that cow!"

77. The Wise Old Rooster — A farmer brought home a new, young rooster to replace his old one because he didn't feel the old rooster could do the job any longer. When the old rooster saw the younger one arrive, he went up to him and said, "Welcome. How about leaving me four hens and you can take the rest?" The young rooster said, "No, I want them all." "How about giving me just one hen?" asked the old rooster. "No, not even one," replied the young rooster. "Well, before I leave, how about racing me around the barnyard a couple of times?" queried the old rooster. "Okay, I'll do that," said the younger one. "And since I'm old, how about giving me a head start," asked the older one. "Okay," said the young rooster. So they started racing around the barnyard. The second time around, as they passed the farmhouse, the farmer came out with a shotgun and shot the younger rooster dead. As he turned to go back inside, the farmer was heard to say, "I can't believe it, that's the third queer rooster I've bought in three weeks."

78. The Facts Of Life — A father called his 12-year-old son aside one day and said, "Son, don't you think it's time we talked about the facts of life?" The son said, "Yes, it is Dad. What is it you'd like to know?"

79. The Atheist — There was a college professor who was an avowed atheist and a showoff. One day in class, he said he'd proved there was no God. He stood on the platform and loudly said, "God, if you are real, knock me off this platform. I'll give you 15 minutes." The lecture room fell silent. After a few minutes, the professor said, "Here I am God, I'm still waiting." After ten minutes, a new member of the class, a newly-released Marine, got out of his seat, walked forward, and hit the professor full in the face, knocking him off the platform and out. The young Marine then calmly took his seat. When the professor regained consciousness he said to the Marine, "Why did you do that?" The Marine responded, "God was busy—he sent me."

80. **The Full Load** — A substitute preacher arrived at a small, country church to find that the only person in attendance was a local farmer who came in his bib overalls. The preacher debated whether to give his full sermon and decided he should give it all. He preached for over an hour, and after the service he asked the farmer how he liked the sermon. The farmer responded by saying, "You know, if I had a wagon full of hay and took it out to the pasture, and found only one cow there, I wouldn't give him the full load."

81. **The Clerical Collar** — A visiting pastor wearing a clerical collar was giving the children's sermon in front of the church. He decided to ask the children if anyone knew why he wore the clerical collar. There was silence until a little girl in the back stood up and said she knew. "Okay," said the pastor, "why do I wear it?" "Because it prevents fleas and ticks for up to five months," said the little girl.

82. **The Repeated Sermon** - A new pastor arrived to take over a church. He became overwhelmed with his new duties, having several funerals and weddings, and meeting and visiting with the new congregation. As a result, he didn't have time to prepare new sermons, so he preached the same sermon four Sundays in a row. The elders were upset at this and went to the bishop with responsibility for the pastor. They complained that he had preached the same sermon over and over four times. The bishop asked, "What was the sermon about?"

None of the elders could remember and there was silence. Finally, the bishop said, "I think he should be able to preach it one more time."

83. The Good and Bad News — One Sunday the pastor said to his congregation, "I have good and bad news for you. The good news is that we have all the money we need to build our new church. The bad news is the money is still in your pockets."

84. The Missing Page — A minister was used to reading his sermons word for word, page after page. One of his parishioners decided to try and cure him of the practice, so one Sunday he slipped up to the pulpit and pulled one of the pages out of the pile before the service. The pastor was reading the sermon when he came to the missing page. Just before he turned the page he was reading about the garden of Eden, "And Adam said to Eve . . . and Adam said to Eve . . . Oh my, there seems to be a leaf missing!"

85. Mrs. Billy Graham — A reporter was interviewing Mrs. Billy Graham about their long marriage and finally asked her, "Did you ever in your long marriage consider divorce?" Mrs. Graham thought for a moment and then said, "Divorce no, never. Homicide, maybe, but not divorce."

86. Rule of Thumb — A theology professor was giving advice to some seminary students. He said there is one golden rule you should follow when you are preaching and that is: "If you haven't struck ore after 10 minutes, stop boring."

87. The Frog — A pastor was giving a children's sermon and asked the children to tell him what he was about to describe. He said, "What is green, lives in ponds, sits on lily pads, and hops about?" A little girl in the back stood up and said, "It sounds a lot like a frog, but it must be Jesus."

88. The Wedding — A minister of a large church had agreed to marry a couple following the Sunday morning sermon. When he finished the service, he was about to call the couple forward, but he had forgotten their names, so he finally said, "Would those who would like to be married please come forward." Three widows, nine single ladies, four widowers, and six single men went to the front of the church.

89. **The False Teeth** — A minister preached a short, ten-minute sermon and was asked afterward why it was so short. He said, "I had a terrible toothache and just couldn't go on." The minister had his teeth pulled and got false teeth. This seemed to solve the problem and his sermons were routinely 20 to 25 minutes long. One Sunday, however, the sermon went on for over an hour. One of the elders asked him why he preached so long. The pastor replied that morning he had taken the wrong false teeth out of the jar and got his wife's dentures instead of his own, and he just couldn't stop them from talking.

90. **The Poor Preacher** — A little boy went up to their pastor and said that when he grew up he was going to give him a lot of money. The pastor was flattered and asked the little boy why he would be so kind. The little boy said, "Because my dad said you are the poorest preacher we have ever had."

91. **The Good Deed** — Two years after World War II ended, a Dutchman in Amsterdam went to his priest and said, "Father, forgive me for I have sinned." "What have you done, son?" asked the priest. "I hid a man in my attic so the Germans wouldn't get him." "That's not a sin," said the priest, "that's a good deed." "But I got him to agree to pay me 20 guilders a week to stay there," said the Dutchman. "Well, that's not too good, but you still did a good deed," replied the priest. As the man started to leave, he turned to the priest and said, "Father, one last question. Should I tell him the war is over?"

92. The Dog Burial — A good Irish Catholic man named Muldoon had a dog that was his long-time companion, and the dog died. He went to the priest and asked if he could have a burial service for the dog in the church. The priest said they didn't have funerals for dogs and that he should try a new church in town that had some funny practices. He said he thought they might bury dogs. Muldoon then said, "Father, do you think paying them $20,000 for the service would be too much?" The priest quickly responded, "Maybe we can work something out here—you didn't tell me the dog was a Catholic."

93. The Heavenly Rewards — A priest and a taxi driver arrived at the pearly gates and asked to enter. Saint Peter welcomed them and said, "Follow me." He took them to a beautiful mansion and told the taxi driver that this was to be his home. He then took the priest to a small shack with two rooms and told him that was his reward. The priest became upset and said, "This isn't fair. I served you as a priest and get a shack, and you give the taxi driver a mansion. How come?" Saint Peter responded, "Well, down on earth when you preached, the people slept. When people got into the taxi cab, they all began to pray."

94. The Bad Boys — Two brothers, eight and 11 years old, were the scourge of a little, Midwestern town. They were always in trouble. Their mother didn't know what to do with them. When a new pastor came to town, she decided to see if he could help, so she decided to send them one at a time for counseling. When the eight-year-old met with the pastor, he said to the boy in a booming voice, "Where is God?" The little boy was frightened and didn't answer. Again the pastor asked, "Where is God?" The little boy was now petrified, and when the pastor again boomed out, "Where is God?" he raced out of the office and into his house and hid in a closet. When his 11-year-old brother found him the younger one said, "Boy, now we're in deep trouble. God's missing, and they think we're responsible."

95. **The Dying Pastor** — A popular preacher was dying, and he sent for a prominent banker and lawyer to come to his side. While neither the banker nor lawyer attended church, they thought it was an honor to be asked to come to the pastor's side in his dying hour. When they came to the pastor's bedroom, he asked one to sit on each side of his bed. Finally, the banker asked the pastor why he had asked them to come. The pastor, who was very weak, finally summoned up his last breath and said weakly, "I wanted to die like my Master, Jesus, between two thieves."

96. **The Duck and the Grapes** — A duck walked into a drug store and asked the pharmacist if he had any grapes. The pharmacist said he didn't, but the grocery store down the street probably had them. The next day the duck came in again and asked once more if he had any grapes. The pharmacist, a bit perturbed, said, "No," and again directed the duck to the grocery store. The third day the duck came in and asked for grapes and the pharmacist blew up, and said, "If you ever come in and ask for grapes again, I'll nail your webbed feet to the floor." The fourth day the duck came in and asked if the pharmacist had any nails. The pharmacist said, "No," whereupon the duck replied, "Well then, do you have any grapes?"

97. **The Spell Check** — After a long illness, a lady died and arrived at the pearly gates. She asked Saint Peter if she could come in and he said, "You may come in if you will spell a word for me." "What word?" she asked. Saint Peter said, "Spell love for me." The woman did so and was admitted to heaven. One day Saint Peter had some business in another part of heaven and asked the woman if she would mind taking his place for a time at the pearly gate, which she did. While there, her husband arrived from earth. The woman asked how he had been. He said he'd been fine, that he had married the pretty nurse who had attended her, had won the lottery, had sold their house and bought a mansion, had traveled all over the world with his new wife, and had been killed in a skiing accident. "So, how do I get into heaven?" her husband asked. "You must spell one word,"

his wife answered. "What word?" he inquired. "Czechoslovakia," she responded.

98. The Old Man — An old man was eating in a diner when three Hells Angels came in and began to pick on him. One tipped his glass of milk over, another put his cigarette out in his pie, and the third poured water on his sandwich. The man said nothing, paid his check, and left the diner. One of the motorcyclists said to the waitress, "That isn't much of a man, is he?" "No," she said, "and he's not much of a driver either because his truck just ran over three motorcycles."

99. The Twins — A woman had twins and was forced to put them up for adoption. One was named Juan and was sent to Spain, and the other was named Amahl and went to Egypt. The woman tried to keep in touch with the boys, and years later, she finally got a picture of Juan in the mail. She said to her husband, "I have a picture of Juan; I also want to get one of Amahl." Her husband replied, "Why? They're twins; if you've seen Juan you've seen Amahl." (Sorry!)

100. The Nameless Tombstone — A young boy was given a horrible name at birth by his father. He named the boy Odd. All throughout his life the boy struggled with his name. People poked fun of him and laughingly asked him if he "was Odd." Poor Odd put up with it all, but when he was older and about to die, he asked his wife if she would do him one last favor. He asked her to put a tombstone on his grave that would omit the horrible name he had to live with all his life. He asked her to just put the dates of his birth and death on the stone and omit his name. His wife agreed, and after his death she placed a beautiful stone marker on his grave, which was near a major walkway in the cemetery. Now when people walk by the stone, they look at it, see no name, and say . . . . "Isn't that odd?" (Sorry again.)

101. The Bible Story — A man was telling his son about the Bible story of Lot. He said, "Because of the sin of Sodom, God told Lot to take his wife and flee." He then told his son about how Lot's wife turned back and became a pillar of salt. The little boy thought for a moment and then said, "What happened to the flea?"

102. **The Confessional** — A new priest arrived at a parish and had some concerns about hearing confessions, so he asked an older priest if he would observe him and give him some suggestions. After observing the young priest, the older one took him aside and said, "I have some suggestions. As the people confess, try crossing your arms and rub your chin with one hand. Also, try saying, 'Yes, I see, go on, and I understand how you feel.'" The young priest went back and heard some more confessions and returned to the older priest. The older priest then said, "Now, isn't that better than slapping your knee and saying, 'No way! What happened next?'"

103. **The Big Lie** — A pastor told his congregation that he was going to preach a sermon the next Sunday on lying, and he asked each member to read Mark 17 in preparation. The next Sunday, as he began his sermon, the pastor asked how many in the congregation had read Mark 17, as he had requested. Nearly every hand in the audience went up, whereupon the pastor said, "There is no Mark 17. I will now proceed to my sermon on lying."

104. **The Exercise Class** — An elderly lady, who was very much overweight went to her doctor and got permission to join an exercise class. She decided to join an aerobics class. After the first class, she said to her doctor, "I bent, twisted, gyrated, jumped up and down, and perspired for an hour, but by the time I got my leotards on, the class was over."

105. **The Funeral Home** — An elderly lady was at a funeral home working out arrangements to bury her 97-year-old husband. The funeral director asked her how old she was. She answered, "I'm a year older than my husband, I'm 98. It's hardly worth going home, is it?"

106. **The Shoppers** — An elderly woman decided to talk to a funeral director to plan ahead for her funeral. She said she'd like to be cremated and to have her ashes spread over the roof of the local Wal-Mart store. The funeral director said, "Why on earth would you want your ashes spread on the roof of the Wal-Mart? The lady replied, "Then I know my daughters will visit me at least twice a week."

107. **The Hot Flashes** — Two elderly ladies were talking about their problem with hot flashes. One said to the other, "Don't think of them as hot flashes, think of them as your inner child playing with matches."

108. **The Speeding Senior** — An elderly lady was pulled over for speeding and the officer asked her for her driver's license. She said she didn't have one since it had been revoked for drunk driving. He then asked her for the car's registration. The lady indicated she didn't have one since she stole the car the day before. She also indicated that she killed the former owner, hacked up his body, and put it in the trunk. At this, the police officer rushed to his car and called for backup. Soon five police cars arrived. A senior police officer with his gun drawn asked the lady to step out of her car. The lady stepped out and said, "Is there a problem, officer?" The senior officer said, "One of my officers said you have stolen this car and murdered the owner. Would you please open the trunk?" The woman opened the trunk, revealing that nothing was there. The officer said, "Is this your car?" The woman replied it was and showed him the registration. The officer then said, "My officer said you didn't have a valid driver's license." Upon hearing this, the elderly lady produced her driver's license." The senior officer then said, "I can't understand this. One of my best officers said that you were driving a stolen car without a drivers license, and that you had murdered the owner and put him in the trunk." The woman then replied, "I'll bet the liar told you I was speeding too didn't he?"

109. **The Convert** — Many years ago, when Catholics couldn't eat fish on Fridays, a Lutheran farmer in the Midwest, named Ole, retired and moved to a small, rural town. It turned out that he was the only Protestant in the town which was over 99% Catholic. It also turned out Ole loved his steaks and cooked every Friday night on an outside grill, sending the smell of cooking steaks wafting over the town. The Catholic priest decided the only way to remove the temptation from his members and solve the problem was to convert Ole to Catholicism. At first Ole resisted, but he finally gave in. On the morning he was admitted to the Catholic Church the priest placed his hand on Ole's head and said, "Born a Lutheran, raised a Lutheran, now a Catholic." The priest figured he had solved his problem, until the next Friday when again the smell of cooking steaks spread across the small town. The priest hurried over to Ole's house, and as he rounded the corner of the house he saw Ole standing over three steaks on the grill, with his hand over them saying, "Born a cow, raised a cow, now a fish."

110. **The Guests In Hell** — Billy Graham, the pope, and Oral Roberts were on an airplane that crashed and all were killed. The three arrived at the pearly gates and Saint Peter said they weren't prepared for them because they didn't know they were coming. He said it would be a week or two before their mansions would be ready, and he wondered if they would mind staying in hell for a few days. They agreed, so Saint Peter called Lucifer and asked if they could come down for a short time. Two days later, Lucifer called Saint Peter and said, "You've got to come and get these guys. The pope is pardoning everybody, Billy Graham is converting everybody, and Oral Roberts has raised so much money we can now air condition the place."

111. **The Improving Creator** — George Younce, the famous base singer of the Cathedral's Quartet, was fond of telling a story about his young granddaughter. She was sitting on his lap one day and ran her hand over his wrinkled face. She then asked him, "Did God

make you, Grandpa?" "Yes, he did," George responded. The little girl then ran her fingers over her smooth facial skin and said, "And did God make me, too, Grandpa?" "Yes, he did," George responded. The little granddaughter thought for a moment and then said, "He's really getting better at it, isn't he."

112. **The Moped and the Harley** — One day, an 80-year-old man on a small, green moped pulled up alongside a member of the Hells Angels motorcycle gang sitting on a beautiful Harley-Davidson motorcycle. The elderly man asked if he could take a closer look at the beautiful motorcycle. The bearded Hells Angel said he could. When he finished, the Hells Angel decided to impress the old man, so he revved up the engine and took off as fast as he could. Within three seconds, he was doing 70 mph. A second or two later, he looked in his rearview mirror and saw the old man on the green moped gaining on him, going twice as fast. The old man passed him and then slowed down, turned around, and went past him again in the other direction. The Hells Angel looked in his rear view mirror again only to see the green moped turn around once more and come flying at him. This time the moped hit him, sending both vehicles into a nearby ditch. The motorcyclist got up, dusted himself off, and saw the 80-year-old man lying in the ditch, and took pity on him. He said to the old man, "Is there anything I can do for you?" "Yes," said the old man, "Please unhook my suspenders from your handlebar."

113. **Palm Sunday** — A little boy was sick one Palm Sunday so he couldn't go to church. When his parents came home, they each held a beautiful palm branch. The little boy asked them what they were holding. They said these were palm branches and that people had put them in Jesus' path as he passed by. The little boy responded, "Wouldn't you know that the first Sunday I'm sick, Jesus shows up."

114. **The Easter Egg** — During the children's sermon, the pastor took out a large Easter Egg and asked the children if anyone knew

what was in the egg. A little boy in the back piped up and said he knew—it had to be a pair of pantyhose.

115. **Life after Death** — A man decided to get some time off from work, so he told his boss that he had to attend his grandmother's funeral. When he returned to work, his boss came up to him and said he marveled at the miracle. "What miracle?" asked the employee, "Why, your grandmother was raised from the dead," said his boss. "She stopped in to see you just a few hours after you left for her funeral."

116. **The Cost of a Sermon** — One morning, a pastor got up before the congregation and announced he had three sermons he could preach that day. He said he had one five minutes long that would cost $1,000, and another for 15 minutes that would cost $500, and a third for $100 which would last for an hour. He then said, "We will now take up the collection to see which one I will preach."

117. **The Band-Aid** — A pastor with a reputation for preaching lengthy sermons showed up for church one Sunday morning with a Band-Aid on his chin. He announced he had cut his chin shaving that morning while thinking about his sermon. A loud voice from the back of the church was heard to say, "Why didn't you think about your chin and cut your sermon."

118. **Elijah's Cookout** — A third grade Sunday school teacher was telling her class about the story of Elijah, the priests of Baal, and the contest on Mount Carmel. After telling how the priests of Baal were unable to call down fire on their sacrifice, she told how Elijah prepared to sacrifice an ox by placing it on the altar. The teacher then told of how Elijah asked his followers to pour water on the ox. Next, the teacher posed the a question to the class: "Why would Elijah have his followers pour water on the sacrifice?" A little girl at the back of the room raised her hand and said, "I know, because Elijah wanted to make gravy."

119. The Cross — A little, four-year-old girl was sitting in church with her mother and she said with a sad voice, "Mother, did Jesus die on the cross?" "Yes," her mother said, and she quickly added, to make her daughter feel better, "But he arose from the dead." The little girl then said, "The next time he should be more careful."

120. The Names of Jesus — A little, four-year-old boy came home from Sunday school and told his parents they were studying the different names of Jesus. His father asked what name they had studied that day. The little boy responded, "Alfalfa and Omega."

121. The Garden of Eden — Adam was walking by the Garden of Eden one day with his sons, Cain and Abel. Abel said, "What's that Daddy?" Adam responded, "That's the Garden of Eden. We used to live there." "Why did we leave," asked Cain. "Because your mother ate us out of house and home," Adam replied.

122. The Haircut — A minister was preaching on and on when he noticed one of his parishioners get up and leave. The preacher continued to preach, and about a half hour later, the parishioner returned. After the service, the pastor asked the man why he had left. "Was there an emergency?" the pastor asked. "No, I went to get a haircut," the man replied. "Well, couldn't you have gotten a haircut before the service?" asked the pastor. "I didn't need it then," replied the man.

123. Failure of Geritol — Many years ago, they produced a supposed miracle drug called Geritol. During that time it is said the following newspaper item appeared. "Today Geritol had its first failure. A 99-year-old woman who had been taking it died—but they did save her baby."

124. Jonah and Whales — An elementary school class was having a lesson on whales. A little girl spoke up and said Jonah had been swallowed by a whale. The teacher said that probably did not happen because, while whales are large animals, they have very small throats. The little girl then said, "When I get to heaven, I will ask Jonah." The teacher then said, "What if Jonah isn't in heaven? What if he went to hell?" "Then you ask him," replied the little girl.

125. **Circulation of Blood** — An elementary teacher was teaching her children about the circulation of blood. To illustrate, she asked the children what would happen to her blood if she stood on her head. One child said the blood would rush to her head and her face would become red. "Yes," the teacher replied, "that's correct. And why doesn't the blood run into my feet?" A little boy in the back responded, "Because your feet aren't empty."

126. **The Class Picture** — An elementary teacher was trying to get her class to buy copies of their class picture. She said, "Won't it be nice when you're all grown up to say, 'There's John—he's now a successful lawyer. And there's Jane—she's a wonderful college professor.'" A small voice at the back of the room spoke up and said, "And there's the teacher, she's dead."

127. **White Hairs** — A little girl noticed one day that her mother had a couple of white hairs. She asked her mother, "How did you get those white hairs, Mother?" The mother said, "Well, every time you don't obey me or you're naughty, I get a white hair." The little girl thought for a moment and then said, "You must have been really bad as a little girl because Grandma's hair is all white."

128. **Pet Names** — A young couple moved into a new neighborhood and were invited to dinner by their neighbors, an 80-year-old couple. During dinner, the young couple noticed the elderly gentleman called his wife by a series of pet names. Every time she brought something to the table, or passed something, he'd say thank you, "wonderful," or "sweetheart," or "gorgeous," or "beautiful." After dinner, the two men were talking and the younger one said to the other, "I'm really impressed by how much you love your wife and

146 •   L. James Harvey

express it by calling her all those pet names." The older gentleman replied, "Well, it's not that I love her that much, it's just that about ten years ago I forgot her name."

129. **The Talking Bills** — A $50 bill and a $1 bill found themselves together in a cash register and began to talk to each other. The $1 bill said to the other, "Where have you been lately?" The $50 bill said, "Well, I've been to Macy's, to a casino, and to a bar downtown. How about you? Where have you been?" The $1 bill said, "I've been to some churches lately." "What's a church?" replied the $50 bill.

130. **The Counselor's Advice** — A husband and wife went to see a counselor after 15 years of marriage. When the counselor asked about their problem, the wife launched into a tirade, listing every problem they had in 15 years. She went on and on. Finally, the counselor got up, walked around the desk, hugged the wife, and kissed her passionately. The woman shut up and sat quietly in a daze. The counselor then turned to the husband and said, "This is what your wife needs at least three times a week. Can you do this? The husband thought for a moment and then replied, "Well, I can drop her off here on Mondays and Wednesdays, but on Fridays I go fishing."

131. **The Three Legged Chicken** — A couple was driving down a country road when a three-legged chicken came alongside. They sped up, but the chicken kept up with them. They sped up again but the chicken easily kept pace. Finally, the chicken passed them and turned into a farmhouse driveway. The couple followed the chicken and parked their car. The farmer came out and the couple asked if he had seen a three legged chicken. He said, "Oh, yes we bred him. You see we have three of us here and we all like drumsticks. So we bred a three-legged chick so we'd only have to kill one chicken for a dinner." "Well, how do the drum sticks taste?" asked the couple. "We don't know," said the farmer, "We've never been able to catch one of the chickens."

More Examples of Clean Humor

In closing this section, let me list some biblical interpretations I received over the Internet. They are taken from papers submitted by children in a Catholic elementary school who were asked to respond to certain biblical questions. These are their actual statements, including their misspellings. Here then are their responses to questions about the New and Old Testaments:

1. Adam and Eve were created from an apple tree. Noah's wife was called Joan of Ark. Noah built an ark, which animals came to in pears.

2. Sampson slayed the Philistines with the axe of the apostles.

3. Moses led the Hebrews to the Red Sea where they made unleavened bread, which is bread without any ingredients.

4. The Egyptians were all drowned in the dessert. Afterwards, Moses went up on Mount Cyanide to get the ten amendments.

5. The first commandment was when Eve told Adam to eat the apple.

6. The seventh commandment is thou shalt not admit adultery.

7. Moses died before he ever reached Canada. Then Joshua led the Hebrews in the battle of Geritol.

8. The greatest miracle in the Bible is when Joshua told his son to stand still and he obeyed him.

9. David was a Hebrew king skilled at playing the liar. He fought with the Finklesteins, a race of people who lived in Biblical times.

10. Solomon, one of David's sons, had 300 wives and 700 porcupines.

11. When Mary heard that she was the mother of Jesus, she sang the Magna Carta.

12. When the three wise guys from the east side arrived, they found Jesus in the manager.

13. Jesus was born because Mary had and immaculate contraption.

14. Jesus enunciated the Golden Rule, which says to do to others before they do one to you. He also explained a man doth not live by sweat alone.

15. The people who followed the lord were called the 12 decibels.

16. The epistles were the wives of the apostles.

17. One of the opossums was Saint Matthew who was also a taxi man.

18. Saint Paul cavorted to Christianity. He preached holy acrimony, which is another name for marriage.

19. Christians have only one spouse. This is called monotony.

Parting thought: Remember you don't stop laughing because you're old; you grow old because you stop laughing.

Appendix B
Is Holy Laughter Holy?

There is a phenomenon in Christianity, particularly in the Pentecostal and Charismatic sectors of the faith, which needs to be addressed in a book on Christian humor. This phenomenon is called "holy laughter," and it is very controversial.

Before going forward, it is important to define clearly what we mean by "holy laughter." I'm referring here to the phenomenon whereby a person breaks out in an uncontrollable fit of laughter. The fact that it is uncontrollable is important, as we shall see. The laughter in the Christian context takes place when a person is having a religious experience and/or is participating in a religious service, usually a revival service.

This subject is approached with great hesitancy because the controversy over holy laughter divides well-meaning Christians with strong opinions on both sides. I would have gladly avoided writing about it altogether, if it were possible. But I finally came to the conclusion that one could not write a book on God and laughter with integrity and not touch on the subject of holy laughter.

In dealing with this subject, I searched the scriptures and read a great deal of material both pro and con. There were numerous articles and books written on the topic, particularly in the late 1990s when the phenomenon attracted worldwide attention. If the reader wishes to read more on the subject, there is a list books at the end of this chapter that will provide further information. It is also possible to find a list of articles on the subject by going to an Internet search engine, like Google, and entering "holy laughter" as a topic.

The hesitancy to write on this subject comes from scriptural admonishments not to judge, lest we be judged. Jesus himself makes this point (Matthew 7:1). Jesus also indicates in Mark 3:29 that the unpardonable sin is to blaspheme against the Holy Spirit. In short, to call the working of the Holy Spirit the work of the devil is perhaps the most serious sin one can commit. On the other hand, we are also told in scripture that false teachers will come (Matthew 7:15). We are warned that particularly in the latter days, false teachers will come and lead many astray (Matthew 24:11, 24; Mark 13:11; II Peter 2:1; I John 4:6). We are admonished by the apostle Paul to have discernment so we can separate God's work and the Holy Spirit's activity from that of the evil one. In fact, in I Corinthians 12:10, Paul indicates one of the gifts of the Holy Spirit is the "ability to distinguish between spirits." We are all well-advised to search scriptures diligently so that we will be able to separate truth from error as the Bereans were praised for doing in Acts 17:11.

So it is with the a prayer for guidance that I proceed with the following critique of the holy laughter phenomenon.

Holy laughter is uncontrolled laughter that can last for hours and lead to complete exhaustion, with people often falling down to sleep or in a trance for some time until they recover. In a religious service, holy laughter is often accompanied by other manifestations, such as people who bark like a dog, howl and roar like animals, hoot like owls, moo like cows, hop about like kangaroos, hiss and crawl about like snakes, and make other noises. People often run about and dance, and fall into trances as well. Holy laughter may appear by itself, but it is most often in conjunction with these other phenomenon. In theses services, people also often speak in tongues (glossolalia), have healing experiences, are "slain in the spirit," and report being touched by the Holy Spirit.

While I am critical of holy laughter and some of the other theatrics in these services, it is important to note I also believe that some speaking in tongues is a valid manifestation of the Spirit, that healing can take place, and that the salvation message can be proclaimed and people saved in these services, even when artificial enhancements are used. God can even use imperfect activities for his purposes.

The phenomenon of holy laughter has historical roots. However, it has been popularized and spread in recent years primarily by a South African evangelist named Rodney Howard-Browne. Holy laughter has also played an important role in a revival movement focusing on a church near the Toronto Airport, called by many the Toronto Blessing (TB). The phenomenon has spread around the world, with particularly strong manifestations in England, Australia, and New Zealand, where Rodney Howard-Browne has preached.

Holy laughter is considered by many to be a manifestation of the presence of the Holy Spirit and a sign of God's touch on a life. By others it is considered possession of a person by a demon or unholy spirit. Is it of God or of Satan? That is the question which needs to be answered.

Instances of holy laughter are reported as early as the 1730s by John Wesley, and the experience has been reported in Africa and India in events not connected to the Christian faith. In his journal, John Wesley reports the following: (from *The Journal of the Rev. John Wesley*, A.M., Vol. 2, London, England: The Epworth Press, 1938. Edited by Nehemiah Curmock.):

Friday 9th May 1740 "I was a little surprised at some who were buffeted of Satan in an unusual manner, by such a spirit of laughter as they could in no wise resist, though it was pain and grief to them. I could scarce have believed the account they gave me, had I not known the same thing 10 or 11 years ago. Part of Sunday my brother and I then used to spend walking in the meadows and singing psalms. But one day, just as we were beginning to sing, he burst out into a loud laughter. I asked him if he was distracted, and began to be very angry, and presently to laugh as loud as he. Nor could he possibly refrain, though we were ready to tear ourselves in pieces, but we were forced to go home without singing another line."

Note here that the laughter came upon John and Charles Wesley suddenly and it interrupted their singing and praising God. Here's another entry from John Wesley's Journal:

Wednesday 21st May 1740 "In the evening such a spirit of laughter was among us that many were offended. But the attention of all was fixed on poor Lucretia Smith whom we all knew to be no dissembler. One so violently and variously torn of the evil one did I never see before. Sometimes she laughed till almost strangled; then broke into cursing and blaspheming; then stamped and struggled with incredible strength, so that four or five could scarce hold her: Then cried out, 'Oh, eternity, eternity! Oh, that I had no soul! Oh, that I had never been born!' At last she faintly called on Christ to help her. And the violence of her pangs ceased. Most of our brethren and sisters were now fully convinced that those who were under this strange temptation could not help it. Only Elizabeth Brown and Anne Holto were of another mind, being sure anyone might help laughing if she would. This they declared to many on Thursday: but on Friday, 23 God suffered Satan to teach them better. Both of them were suddenly seized in the same manner as the rest, and laughed whether they would or no, almost without ceasing. Thus they continued for two days, a spectacle to all; and were then upon prayer made for them, delivered in a moment" (Wesley, 1938, 347).

Notice that Wesley considered holy laughter as satanic and unspiritual. Also note that the phenomenon ended without exception when prayer to God was offered to stop it. In addition, it is important to note that a believer, Lucretia Smith, when possessed by the laughter, suddenly turned to cursing and blaspheming, hardly something one would do under the influence of the Holy Spirit. It's significant also, that in the case of John and Charles, as well as Lucretia and the other two ladies, the holy laughter came spontaneously upon believers and it interrupted ongoing religious activities.

Holy laughter has been a significant factor in two major revivals in churches in North America in the late 20th century. One revival occurred in the Brownsville Assembly of God Church near Pensacola, Florida. The other, as mentioned earlier, was at the Toronto Airport Vineyard Church in Canada. The Brownsville revival began in June 1995 and the Toronto revival began in January 1994.

Holy laughter became a major focus of the Toronto revival but was considered a diversion in the Brownsville revival. Both revivals have drawn people to their services from all over the world. In Toronto, some excesses in holy laughter and related manifestations of the spirit, mentioned above, and some other issues actually led to a split in the church from its parent organization, the Vineyard International Consortium. A representative of the Brownsville Assembly of God Church told this writer that while they had some manifestations of the Holy Spirit and also had holy laughter, they refused to allow the holy laughter to interrupt their services; people who laughed were asked to leave. Representatives from the headquarters of the Assembly of God Church have visited Brownsville and have put their stamp of approval on the revival there. It is interesting to note that where holy laughter was fully accepted and given full reign as a manifestation of the Holy Spirit, along with the attendant manifestations, the revival was fractured and the church hosting it was split from its denomination. In Brownsville, they controlled

154 • L. James Harvey

holy laughter, refused to allow it to disrupt the services, and they have continued their revival without division. In one it helped divide a church while in the other it was not allowed to become divisive.

When one examines scripture, there is no mention of the phenomenon of holy laughter. It is nowhere listed as a gift of the spirit, nor noted anywhere in connection with the apostles and other early Christians who were clearly under the influence of the Holy Spirit. For example, speaking in tongues, rejoicing in the spirit, speaking in foreign languages, etc. are mentioned at Pentecost, but not uncontrollable laughing.

In 1979, in Port Elizabeth, South Africa, a young man by the name of Rodney Howard-Browne was frustrated in not having a more significant religious experience and reportedly cried out to God, "Either you come down here and touch me, or I'll come up there and touch you." Browne reports he felt God touch him, and from that time on, he became an evangelist and the leading proponent of the concept of holy laughter. It became a trademark of his meetings. He then brought it to America. One of those who became convinced it was an outpouring of the Holy Spirit was John Arnott, pastor of the Toronto Airport Vineyard Church. Holy laughter there, too, became a trademark for their "visitation of the spirit" and a hallmark of many of their revival services.

In 1980, there was a report that the phenomenon of holy laughter had occurred in a revival meeting Jimmy Swaggert was having in Argentina. The laughter interrupted the meeting and the people had to be taken outside because it was disturbing the meeting.

Differing from normal laughter in several ways, holy laughter:
1. is usually uncontrollable.
2. appears only in a religious context.
3. is most often accompanied by other manifestations like barking, howling, and others.

4. is sometimes facilitated by the touch or other action of the evangelist.
5. seems clearly to be caused by a spirit or demon.
6. can be stopped by prayer in the name of Jesus.
7. usually disrupts a religious service and becomes the focal point of the gathering.
8. appears most often in meetings of select evangelists who advertise the presence of it in their services.

When the holy laughter phenomenon was brought to America by Rodney Howard-Browne, it was welcomed and validated as a true sign of the Holy Spirit by Marilyn Hickey, Kenneth Copeland, John Arnott, and others. The phenomenon was accepted by many charismatics, but particularly by the group which has been categorized as the Word-Faith, Word of Faith, Name-it-claim-it, Health and Wealth, or Positive Confession Christians. In these categories, we generally find names such as Benny Hinn, Kenneth Hagin Jr., Marilyn Hickey, Paul and Jan Crouch, Fred Price, Robert Tilton, Kenneth Copeland, Oral and Richard Roberts, John Avanzini, John Arnott, and Jesse Duplantis. This list is important in analyzing the holy laughter phenomenon because these people and their ministries have some things in common, which I believe can help us evaluate holy laughter. To make things a bit simpler, I will refer to the group above as the Word of Faith Group, or just the WFers.

There are a number of characteristics these pastors and their ministries have in common, which is significant:

A.) Most are multimillionaires, or were before running into moral and legal problems (e.g., Robert Tilton and Benny Hinn have had problems with the IRS, and Tilton went through a difficult divorce). Ken Copeland and the Crouches fly around in private jets and accept salaries well up in the six figures. Fred Price drives a Rolls Royce, and all accept material rewards as a sign of God's blessing on their ministries. The Crouches have telethons that promise people who will send them $1,000 or $2,000 that their debts will be eliminated in a short time by God. They routinely raise $50 million or more in each of these telethons. In short, they tend to place an inordinate emphasis on materialism.

B.) They place a great emphasis on gaining wealth in this life and preach that God will reward people materially for their faith. This has led some to call these ministries the Health and Wealth ministries. They essentially preach that God will give their followers health and wealth if they will send money to the evangelist as a sign of their faith. They carry this idea a step forward by assuming that anyone who is poor lacks faith.

C.) There is a tendency for these ministries to make a god out of man and themselves. They believe Christians are little gods and have made comments like those below. Following each statement is the TV program or magazine where each statement was made.

1. Ken Hagin Sr. (now deceased): "The believer is called Christ … that's what we all are we're Christs." (*The Word of Faith*, December 1980, 14).

2. Ken Copeland: "You don't have God in you, you are one." (Ken Copeland, "The Force of Love," tape #02-0028). Copeland also said that he could have done what Christ did if he (Copeland) had been alive at the time (Ken Copeland, "What Happened from the Cross to the Throne?" tape #02-0017).

3. Benny Hinn: "I am a little Messiah walking on earth"(TBN, *Praise-a-thon*, broadcast November, 1990).

4. Paul Crouch: "I am a little God! Critics be gone" (TBN, *Praise the Lord*, broadcast July 7, 1986).

D.) They communicate a personal egotism and a vanity that is contrary to the humility which the Bible teaches is a primary characteristic of the mature Christian.

I believe that these characteristics demonstrate a lack of spiritual maturity and a misunderstanding of biblical teaching. I further believe this leads these pastors to engage in theatrics and other activities to validate their ministries, which are unbiblical and are harmful to the church of God. It is this immaturity, I believe, which has led some of them to embrace holy laughter as a sign of God's presence in their services.

Let's take a look at a couple of the issues above in the light of scripture, Christ's example, and other leading Christians of our day. First, regarding humility, we read in Ephesians 4:2, "Be completely humble and gentle; be patient, bearing one another in love." Or in I Peter 5:5, "God opposes the proud but gives grace to the humble." In Matthew 18:4 Jesus says, "Therefore, whoever humbles himself like this child is the greatest in the kingdom of heaven." In Colossians 3:13 we read, "Therefore as God's chosen people, holy and dearly beloved, cloth yourselves with compassion, kindness, humility, gentleness, and patience." Proverbs 15:33 says, "The fear of the Lord teaches a man wisdom and humility comes before honor." In James 3:13 we read, "Do good deeds in humility that comes from wisdom." And lastly, in Philippians 2:3, "Do nothing out of selfish ambition or vain conceit, but in humility consider others better than yourself."

It seems absolutely clear the Bible teaches humility is a cardinal virtue of a Christian, yet it is a quality frequently absent in the WFers. Jesus not only spoke of humility as important but he practiced it himself. He humbled himself to be offered up on the cross. At the Last Supper he demonstrated humility with his disciples by washing their feet. In short, Christ modeled humility for all to see and emulate. In my experience, over a lifetime of meeting Christians of all shapes, sizes, and commitments, the truly great Christians possess a deep humility, which makes them exceptionally approachable and loveable.

If we look at some of the great Christians of our day, we find the same thing. For example, Billy Graham has a right, if any Christian does, to be egotistical about what he has accomplished through his ministry. Instead, we find a deep humility, love, and awe of God. The same could be said of Mother Teresa and Pope John Paul II before their deaths. Other great preachers like the late Bishop Fulton Sheen and the popular TV preacher of today, Charles Stanley, demonstrate humility of biblical character. This humility, by the way, is not evidence of a low self-esteem, weakness, or lack of confidence, but rather recognition that God is far greater than we are, and that we are his children bought for a terrible price. I have also known many less prominent yet deeply committed Christians, and they all are humble people. The WFers seem to lack this quality. They are most often vain in their dress and appearance, live ostentatious lifestyles, and display egos that contradict the humility of biblical teaching.

Another point relates to the matter of wealth. Jesus said in Mark 10:25 (also in Matthew 19:24 and Luke 18:25), "It is easier for a camel to go through the eye of a needle than for a rich man to enter the kingdom of heaven." Jesus himself modeled a modest life and asked his disciples to do the same. The Bible warns in Mark 4:19, 13:22, and Matthew 13:22 about the "deceitfulness of riches." In Proverbs 22:1 "a good name is to be chosen rather than great riches, loving favor rather than silver or gold." It is clear from the Bible and the example of Jesus and his followers, that wealth was not a goal to be sought, and in fact, it posed a great danger to salvation.

I believe we see again in Billy Graham and his ministry team how to handle great fame and riches. Billy and his team early on saw the dangers, and he and his team agreed they would always accept modest salaries rather than accumulate great personal riches, which they easily could have done, given the popularity of their crusades and ministry. This contrasts sharply with the WFers. Not only do the WFers accumulate great personal wealth for themselves, but they use wealth as an enticement for people to support their ministries.

They invariably tempt people by saying God will bless them, take away their debts, and fill their coffers with money if they will just send money to the WFer. They even imply that God will curse those who don't send them money. In short, they hold out wealth as a blessing to their constituents, if they will only send money to their ministry. One of the WFers, Robert Tilton, has been sued and indicted for his shady fundraising practices. That and two divorces have hurt his ministry, but he is still trying to make a comeback using the same tactics he used before.

Brother Andrew, one of the world's outstanding Christians, has always lived modestly and continues to do so today, though his Open Door ministry raises countless millions every year to spread the Gospel in nations where Christians are persecuted. He and many other servants of God like him believe they should follow Christ's model of behavior and not try and emulate the world's success model, which stresses material wealth.

It seems to me that Jesus taught and practiced modesty and frugality, because if a servant of God gets rich from preaching the Gospel, no one can ever be sure whether they are serving God or self. Are they preaching to get wealthy or to spread the truth? Do they believe what they are preaching or preaching to get material riches? No one can be sure, no matter what they say, because the wealth shouts louder than their words.

When Jesus sent out disciples (Luke 10:1-12), he told them not to take even a purse, but rather to live off what believers offered them. The focus was on spreading the Gospel, not on gaining wealth. In the case of Jesus, his disciples, Billy Graham, Brother Andrew, Bishop Fulton Sheen, and a host of other sincere disciples of God, personal wealth was never an issue. Materialism never cast a shadow over their message. The point in all of this is to show that the primary proponents of holy laughter are seemingly inconsistent with some basic biblical principles in their lives and ministries, and while they preach some valid biblical truths, they seem inconsistent in others.

Let me be more specific now regarding holy laughter. My wife and I attended a revival service of Rodney Howard-Browne in Maryland some years ago. We observed the holy laughter, the speaking in tongues, the testimonies of adherents, and the general tenor and tone of the meeting. It was clear that many dear Christians felt the Holy Spirit was in that meeting. We can't with total certainty say that was not the case, but we were not convinced it was the case. The service started with some music and then a talk by Browne. Partway through his talk, the laughing started. From that point on, laughing and speaking in tongues became the focus of the meeting, with some testimonies interspersed.

A good friend of mine, who has a doctor of divinity degree and is a deeply spiritual Christian, attended a three-day pastors' conference held by Rodney Howard-Browne in Florida some years ago. My friend, I should add, very much believes in the gifts of the spirit and in the intervention of the Holy Spirit in human affairs. He tells story after story of how the Holy Spirit has intervened, sometimes dramatically, in his life and ministry. In short, he went to the meeting biased in favor of finding a new work of the Holy Spirit.

My friend came back from the conference feeling the concept of Holy laughter was "plastic and contrived." He also reported that at one point in the conference, the pastors lined up to be "slain in the spirit" by Browne. There were "catchers" behind the pastors. As Browne came down the line, my friend and a colleague waited to see if they would have a spiritual experience. They decided they would not fall backward unless impelled to do so by the Holy Spirit. As Browne pressed his hand on the forehead of each pastor, they would fall backward. When Browne put his hand on my friend, he felt nothing. The "catchers" behind him said, "fall backward." My friend and his colleague felt nothing and refused to fall backward. Browne would undoubtedly say the two were unbelievers who resisted the Holy Spirit. I tend to trust my friend's spirituality more than Browne's.

Rodney Howard-Browne, by the way, claims to have a doctor of ministry degree from the School of Bible Theology Seminary and University (SBTSU) located in San Jacinto, California. It turns out this is a correspondence school offering a range of questionable degrees. When a member of the Christian Research Institute (CRI) called the U.S. Department of Education to check on the school, they were told it was a diploma mill. My visit to the SBTSU Web site revealed that their accreditation comes from the Transworld Accrediting Commission in Riverside California. I have spent over 45 years in higher education in the U.S. and I have never heard of Transworld. It seems Transworld has been set up largely to accredit operations like SBTSU. In short, Browne's educational credentials are very suspect.

The "slain in the spirit" phenomenon, by the way, is another trademark of many WFers, including Browne, and seems to contradict biblical teaching. Nowhere in the Bible do people fall backward under the Holy Spirit's power. We find no evidence that the apostles went about with teams of "catchers" to prevent injury to those slain in the spirit in their meetings. There are numerous examples of people falling on their faces (Ezekiel 3:23, Numbers 16:45, Matthew 17:6, Revelation 7:11, and Revelation 11:16), but no example this writer could find of anyone falling backward, as a result of the positive impact of the Holy Spirit's power. Could it be that the current practice, along with the "catchers," has been devised by the WFers to conform to their high octane meetings and to generate the perception that people are being visited by the Holy Spirit? It's a hypothesis that has some validity, and when coupled with the holy laughter phenomenon, it makes one wonder further about the validity of the WFers and some of their methods.

Let me enter another disclaimer here. I'm not saying every pastor who might be classified as a WFer accepts holy laughter, however, a number do. It also seems clear to the writer that the only pastors who do accept holy laughter are those within the WFer category who also use the theatrics mentioned above, and who have ministries heavily focused on achieving material goals in this life. These pastors seem to more readily accept holy laughter as an evidence of God's presence in their meetings.

Now, before making a definitive statement on holy laughter, I must repeat that I do believe in being moved by the Holy Spirit, I believe in the gifts of the Holy Spirit, I believe in healing, and I believe speaking in tongues is a gift of the Spirit. These things were given to the early church (Acts 2:4 and 10:46). In I Corinthians 14:27, the apostle Paul tells the early church not to prohibit people from speaking in tongues. In this chapter, Paul says he himself spoke in tongues. But he also warns the people about speaking in tongues when unbelievers are present and when there is no interpretation. It is clear that in the early church, as in the church today, in some places speaking in tongues was abused and became a "badge of spiritual merit" rather than a gift of God bringing people closer to the truth.

Having said the above, and being sensitive to the danger of blaspheming against the Holy Spirit, I have come to the conclusion that holy laughter is not holy for the following reasons:

1. There is no biblical example of holy laughter. Nowhere is it mentioned as a gift of the Spirit or a manifestation of the presence of the Holy Spirit.

2. In Galatians 5:22-23, we read that a gift of the Holy Spirit is self-control. When a person is possessed by holy laughter, they are out of control, they can't stop on their own. This is contrary to biblical teaching.

3. Holy laughter is disruptive of worship. A true manifestation of the spirit facilitates worship, it doesn't disrupt it. Note that the Toronto Vineyard Church evidently accepted these disruptions and it led to excesses, which brought conflict in their denomination. The Brownsville revival refused to allow the phenomenon to disrupt their worship, and the unity of the church was preserved.

4. John Wesley, one of the great Christians of the18th century, had a direct encounter with holy laughter and considered it demonic, not a work of the Holy Spirit.

5. The manifestations that accompany holy laughter (barking, acting like animals, etc.) are demonic in nature. There is no evidence anywhere, including in the Bible, that the Holy Spirit would make a person emulate an animal and embarrass themself in such an out-of-control manner.

6. The concept is approved and accepted by a school of evangelists, who themselves seem to espouse some questionable biblical practices. They seem to focus on wealth, when the Bible clearly de-emphasizes it. They also make a god out of man, appearing to go back and make the basic mistake Eve did in the Garden of Eden, namely, wanting to be like God.

7. My personal experience, and that of a good friend, has been that holy laughter is a contrived phenomenon used to seemingly validate the visitation of the Holy Spirit upon a revival meeting.

For all of the above reasons, I have reluctantly come to the conclusion that the holy laughter phenomenon is demonic and appears to be contrary to the true workings of the Holy Spirit. It may well be that the adversary is using this vehicle to lead people astray. It should, in the author's judgment, be viewed with great skepticism.

Let me reiterate a critical point. Having said the above about holy laughter, I am in no way attempting to judge the lives and/or salvation of those who make use of this phenomenon. That is clearly God's job. I only make judgments about the actions of these folks and of the phenomenon in the light of what I know, have experienced, and believe to be true.

If you'd like to read more pro and con regarding holy laughter, below are some books that will be of interest:

1. Arnott, John. *The Father's Blessing*. Lake Mary, Florida: Creation House, 1997.

2. Beverly, James. *Holy laughter and the Toronto Blessing*. Grand Rapids, Michigan: Zondervan, 1995.

3. Brown, Michael L. *From Holy Laughter to Holy Fire*. Shippensburg, Pennsylvania: Destiny Image, 1997.

4. Brown, Michael L. *Let No One Deceive You*. Shippensburg, Pennsylvania: Destiny Image, 1997.

5. Campbell, Wesley. *Welcoming a Visitation of the Holy Spirit*. Nashville, Tennessee: Word Publishing, 1997.

6. Chong, Dr. Eddy. *Deceiving the Elect*. The book is found on the Internet at: www.agape.com/dleappc.htm.

7. Rowdy, Clark. *Lighting Fires*. Lake Mary, Florida: Creation House, 1997.

8. MacArthur, John. *Reckless Faith*. Wheaton, Illinois: Crossway Books, 1994.

About the Author

Dr. L. James Harvey was born and raised in Grand Rapids, Michigan. He is an honors graduate of Hope College in Holland, Michigan and he has MA and Ph.D. degrees from Michigan State University. Dr. Harvey has been a high school teacher and coach, a college dean, vice president, and president, and a senior vice president and partner in an international management consulting firm based in Washington, D.C.

Dr. Harvey has had wide experience in speaking, teaching, and in presenting workshops and seminars throughout the United States and overseas. Speaking largely to college and university faculties and staffs, he gained national recognition as a speaker and consultant in the area of college and university management. He also published several books and articles in his field of expertise.

Dr. Harvey and Jackie, his wife of 56 years, have been active Christian laypersons wherever they have been. Both have been elders, Sunday school teachers, and have held numerous church leadership positions in two denominations, the Reformed Church in America and the Moravian Church in America. Dr. Harvey has also served terms as a trustee on seminary boards in both denominations. They are now members of the Kentwood Community Church in Grand Rapids, Michigan.

Since retirement, Dr. Harvey has begun a new career as a Christian writer and speaker, focusing on matters related to the Christian faith. He has written nine books and has two more in progress.

Further information about Dr. Harvey's books and services is available at these Web sites:

www.sentencesermons.com

www.ReadingUp.com

Other titles from
Dr. L. James Harvey

701 Sentence Sermons
(Grand Rapids, Michigan: Kregel Publications, 2000)

701 More Sentence Sermons
(Grand Rapids, Michigan: Kregel Publications, 2002)

701 Sentence Sermons – Volume 3
(Grand Rapids, Michigan: Kregel Publications, 2005)

701 Sentence Sermons – Volume 4
(Grand Rapids, Michigan: Kregel Publications, 2007)

Every Day Is Saturday
(St. Louis, Missouri: Concordia Publishing House, 2000)
(limited availability)

The Resurrection – Ruse or Reality?
(Baltimore, Maryland: Publish America, 2001)

Letters from Perverse University
(Lincoln, Nebraska: Author's Choice Press, 2001)

Seven For Heaven
(Lima, Ohio: CSS Publishing Company Inc., 2003)

Please visit the author's Web site for ordering information:
www.sentencesermons.com

Available from
Harvest Day Books

$15.95

Jungle Jewels & Jaguars
Living with the Amueshas Translating God's Word
By Martha Tripp

The true story of a young woman's journey deep into the jungles of Peru to live with the native Amuesha tribe, learn their language, and bring to them the Word of God in their native tongue. This amazing memoir brings us the trials and triumphs of this 23-year Bible translation mission.

$15.95

PreScriptures for Life
Praying Scriptures: Allowing God's Word to Renew
By Neil Elmer

Prescriptures for Life is about tapping into God's power to overcome obstacles that get in the way of moving forward in life. This user-friendly book provides pertinent Scripture in a topical format—easy to use and share with a friend. Take your prayer life to a deeper level. This handy reference is great for one-on-one personal ministry.

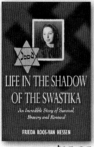

$15.95

Life in the Shadow of the Swastika
An Incredible Story of Survival, Bravery, and Renewal
By Frieda Roos-van Hessen

This powerful, true story recounts the spectacular journey of Frieda as she struggled to survive the Nazi occupation of Holland. As friends and family fell victim to Nazi annihilation, Frieda, along with her friend, Meika, made one death defying escape after another. Experience the emotional rollercoaster as courage, hope, and strength are put to the ultimate test—and salvation of Christ triumphs!

Available from
Harvest Day Books

$12.95

Cleared for Takeoff
50 Stories from the Pen of a Jungle Pilot
50th Anniversary Edition
By Bob Griffin

Veteran missionary aviator, Bob Griffin, shares from his many experiences, beginning with his flight to Ecuador in 1956, where he initiated the aviation program supporting Bible translators. The collection of short stories in this 50th Anniversary Edition are sure to hug your heart and encourage your soul.

$12.95

Together We Can!
A Mosaic of Stories and Devotions Displaying the Impact of God's Word
By Aretta Loving

"*Together We Can!* brings us stories about the truth of God's Word, changed lives, miracles, and increased faith. The one thing they all have in common is the power of the Word of God..."

—Dr. John R. Watters
Executive Director, Wycliffe International

To Place an Order

For additional copies of *Does God Laugh?* or for any title from Harvest Day Books, please visit www.ReadingUp.com. Discounts are available for bulk orders to churches, bookstores, and libraries.

Harvest
Day
Books

Fax orders:	(231)929-1993
Telephone orders:	(231)929-1999
E-mail orders:	orders@bookmarketingsolutions.com
Internet orders:	ReadingUp.com